https://www.backendrising.com
"A voice that needs to be heard", Las Vegas
Public Radio, LLC

HOW YOU'RE BEING MASTURBATED (JERKED AROUND) BY THE U.S. CONSTITUTION

BY SIR ANDREW DEAN LAPORTA

I REALLY FEEL FOR THE LADY IN THE TEA PARTY MOVEMENT, WHO SAID," I WANT MY COUNTRY BACK!"

LADY, IT AINT GONNA HAPPEN!!

AMERICA ALREADY HAS BEEN BOUGHT BY DARWINISM AND THE BRITISH POUND!!!

EVERY AMERICAN SHOULD BE OUTRAGED BY THE CONDUCT, EXERCISED BY OUR GOVERNMENT OFFICIALS FOR THE PAST TWENTY YEARS AND BEYOND!

BY THE AUTHOR,
SIR ANDREW DEAN LAPORTA

SIR ANDREW DEAN LAPORTA IS A SELF
KNIGHTED SERF

BY WE THE PEOPLE, LIVING IN A LAND
ONCE UPON A

TIME CALLED AMERICA THE BEAUTIFUL

SEPERATION OF POWERS A.K.A. (ALSO KNOWN AS) DIVIDING UP

THE LOOT AFTER ROBBING THE TREASURY VIA OVERSEAS INVESTMENTS

CALLED DERIVATIVES, WHICH ARE NOTHING MORE THAN BOND

PURCHASES, DERIVED OUT OF HOT AIR LIKE A HELIUM BALOON, LOFTY,

INTENTIONALLY RIGGED AND CONTROLLED BY THE CORPORATE BOARDS

OF LIBOR JUNK DEALERS TO PICK YOU'RE WALLETS

ABOUT THE AUTHOR

Andrew Dean LaPorta is a multitalented individual who has traveled the world. He is a retired, highly qualified tenured high school teacher under NCLB and funeral director/mortician for 50 years, who lives in Las Vegas, Nevada with his wife Joanne. He has been married for 45 years. In 1963 he was president of his class at Southington High School in Connecticut. He graduated from Southern Connecticut State University with a B.S. and The San Francisco College of Mortuary Science A.M.S . He completed graduate studies in education strategies at workshops at, Oklahoma State University, Yale and Arizona State University. He is an honorable U.S. Navy veteran. Mr. LaPorta was an award winning top producer for the Los Angeles Times Mirror (Hartford Courant affiliate). He also won several awards over a 13 year span with the New Haven Register a Jackson Newspaper. He was president of LaPorta Funeral Home. Most recently, he spent 6 years as a loyal dedicated teacher with commitment to service to the Juvenile Detention School with the Mohave County Arizona Superior Court.

DEDICATION

I would like to dedicate this book to my beautiful, clean hearted, compassionate, mother of my child, wife Joanne, who has been my whole life and bride for over 45 years and whom I love very, very much and to my son Gregory who is the light of the world and the most precious gift this world has yet to know. I love you both, so much.

Also, I would like to honor all the dead war veterans, and their families, who are my real heroes.

In addition, this book is dedicated to all my students, teachers, principals who believed in me and clients who trusted my professionalism.

Most sincerely, to all Eagle Scouts who received throughout the years, The God and Country Award.

This is to all the National Honor Society recipients of awards and scholarships.

To all students of The Daughters of the American Revolution (DAR) who received the award for Excellence in History.

CONTENTS

PREFACE

The Founding Fathers left us with many unanswered questions, due to their inability to sell us an airtight document. This is an electrifying, terse, and diverse calculation of critical thinking by a difference of opinion regarding the structure and intent of the Founders of the U.S. Constitution. The author believes the Constitution has a percentage of which is "notional" meaning roughly "not real" and aims at the heart of the voting electorate –We the people. Its historical look back into the mindset of the Founders is astounding in principle, yet provocative in fact, when fast forwarded in real time to America's problems in 2012. Since, the Founding Fathers were never elected to represent us and were self appointed slave masters who capitalized on the quintessential innocence of the new nation, paid subordinate wages and were allowed to continue with impunity. They have been adulated by a society, that virtually has been screwed by them and held hostage by their power and control. Many questions concerning the responsibility, honesty, integrity, truthfulness, and caring aspects of the Founders are projected through character assassinations, which lead to an upheaval in justice and truth, which are the hallmarks of democracy. Democracy is an illusion according to the writers critique. The questions remain —we are not or will we ever be a British overseas territory? Will we succumb to what the Argentine Falkland Islands have become through globalization- British? The back end of our country is rising up and wants to know what the frack is happening to all of their hard earned money and who and what is controlling their government. The Power and Control of the U.S. by British bankers and no transparency of the private bank known as the umbrella Federal Reserve is exposed as a scam. Our allegedly corrupt Congress is exposed for accepting lobbyist money, that's really a kickback or bribe paid to continue King William I of England's dream of holding onto the monarchy. We have become a "suburb of London" and the Wall Street bankers have taken a script right out of the Queen's playbook.

After the American Revolution "In most states the right to vote was limited to white men who owned property. However, about 70% of the white men in America owned enough property to be able to vote. In contrast, only about 10% of the men were eligible to vote in Great Britain."1

The question is why weren't men eligible to vote in Great Britain? The answer-Power and Control-remember - William the Conquer!

"The basic ideas of natural rights, social content, popular sovereignty, and representation had all been part of the colonial governments. The ideas that the colonists had brought with them from Great Britain."2

So, where did the British get many of their ideas from? The Roman Empire! They plagiarized the Romans, mimicked their customs, ideas, etc. and used the term republican government as their new twist on convincing the praetorian guard to render unto William I, just as the Roman's rendered unto Caesar what is Caesars'----------MONEY! DOUGH-RAE-ME!!

Now, we have come full circle in a little more than 200 years as a nation. The Roman Empire lasted 344 years. Now, the British globalization network is expected by experts to last forever.

Today, Britain has maintained its equity value in the pound by not participating in the European Union "Euro dollars" and only collect interest on Europe's "austerity measures", guaranteeing a "cash out".

The U.S.S. Constitution was our flagship and an important vessel in the U.S. fleet during the War of 1812. The U.S. Constitution as adopted in 1788 is amendable. The question is what are we all waiting for – hell to freeze over – or the wheel of fortune to continue for only the few, who ask you to sacrifice and give your life for the country, while they lick their fingers counting all the casino money from lobbyists?

Question: Why didn't John Adams or Thomas Jefferson sign the Constitution? Perhaps, the government they envisioned wasn't as fascist as what we see today.

PLEDGE OF ALLEGIANCE 2012

I pledge allegiance to the flag of the United States of America and to the REPUBLICANS for which it stands, one DIVIDED nation under God, DIVISIBLE (BECAUSE OF THE GUARANTEED POLICE POWER OVER THE PEOPLE) with Liberty and justice for the elite few, who change the rules whenever they want for themselves and outlaw all other countrymen.

Pledge of Allegiance 2012 (REVISED EDITION)

I PLEDGE ALLEGIANCE TO THE FLAG OF THE UNITED STATES OF AMERICA AND TO THE DEMOCRACY FOR WHICH IT WAS INTENDED, ONE NATION UNDER GOD WITHOUT BRITISH BANKERS RULE OF INFLUENCE, INDIVISIBLE WITH LIBERTY AND JUSTICE FOR ALL.

We have become a "SUBURB OF LONDON" – a city corporation, "business" owned and controlled by private bankers, who live by charging "interest in perpetuity" to the world it wants to dominate. We are not free from the tyranny of the spirit of the dead King George III, nor Queen Elizabeth I, "the killer" of dreams.

In 1577 Queen Elizabeth I who learned there was gold in America, commissioned Francis Drake to go to America and steal the gold from the Mexicans, just like the current Queen, who is really a dictator, but hides behind coined words, called a Constitutional Monarchy, and hides in a Trojan horse and rides with her London crooked bankers daily to suck the cash out of the U.S. Federal Reserve Bank.

CHAPTER 1
NEW BORN BABY IN 2012! AND THE 2012 PREAMBLE TO THE CONSTITUTION OF THE UNITED STATES

The U.S. Constitution is supposed to represent <u>every</u> citizen. By virtually being written by fallible men, it doesn't. The porous cement which was used by the framers is like porism itself (a proposition that unveils the possibility of finding such warrants as to make an itemized problem worthy of many solutions). What the framers left out was justice. They got the structure partially right, but forgot to add the ingredients. Why? Maybe they didn't want to. Why else would they proclaim, what was discussed <u>behind</u> closed doors was not be discussed for 30 years? They would most likely all be dead! Let the next or future generations deal with it! How selfish!! The framers probably would turn over in their graves if they knew how abused every citizen was today. The hurrah for me and frack you attitude echoed by the leaders of Congress today is paramount only to <u>their</u> thinking – Our Way or the Highway!

1

Or Hit The Road Jack And Don't Come Back! More for us and our posterity and less for you --- who cares?!?

Mirror, mirror on the wall, who's the fairest of them all? The Constitution never answers that question. The Constitution is like a new born baby sucking milk from its mother. It is written in such a believable fashion that all the good it is supposed to do is deflated once one grasps realism, that there is no separation of powers and all the Supreme Court Justices are milking the system for life and in bed with their cousins, the Senate who only confirms them!

"The wheels of justice grind slowly, but small". We have all heard of that declaratory sentence. But, really is this one of today's applications? Slowly – yes. But small -hardly.

Water flows downward – the U.S. Constitution is suppose to be our barometer, thermometer, measuring stick, metric stick, etc. Then, why is it working for only a few citizens who can afford representation? There is no stop gap safeguard for freedom in today's America. Ready, aim, fire seems to be the order of the day. When in good conscious, will we ever be in a position to respect our leaders again?

When will "certainty" reestablish itself in our rear view mirrors? Probably, when unselfish men and women are not merely elected to fulfill sacred positions, but who themselves become examples of the values that exceed expectations of their posterity.

The U.S. Constitution is supposed to be the "microcosm" of democracy in action, not democracy "as is to order". Today, we have "super delegates" deciding who should lead us to heaven. Today, "DIRECT DEMOCRACY" is a foregone conclusion as the Electoral College is embedded in its core to maintain "power and control".

2012 PREAMBLE TO THE CONSTITUTION OF THE U.S.

WE THE PEOPLE OF THE U.S.(where is the WE? Our Founding Fathers wrote the Constitution behind closed doors and excluded poor people, women, young people, Native American Indians, free black men or slaves, and indentured servants who paid their way to America.(The delegates to the Philadelphia Convention were not chosen from all parts of the population).

IN ORDER TO FORM A MORE PERFECT UNION, (this is a dream- the founders were racist!- young men, women,blacks, etc. were excluded from voting on anything DUE TO APARTHEID]

ESTABLISH JUSTICE, (for whom? The American Bar Association's web page reads – The American Bar Association, Justice and liberty for all. Yet in real time there isn't a wimper of justice to try and convict the banking crooks who through TARP, gave themselves bonuses with your hard earned money for doing nothing, but cashing the fraudulent checks that Congress gave to them! Where is the justice, when the politically stacked Supreme Court shuts down the 2000 Florida voting count, leaving over 100,000 people out to dry and by a 5 to 4 political vote chose G.W. Bush over Gore, who received more than 500,000 votes? The whole Electoral College is a scam of late. Isn't it funny when the party of "NO" needed to block the 60 vote B.S. majority, that they were still counting votes 9 months later in Minnesota, to hopefully block Al Franken, the Senate candidate from Minnesota, from becoming Senator # 60? But, the 5/4 Supreme Court said, we need to let the system/process work. What a crock of B.S.!! Where is their Justice, when the U.S. SUPREME court enters the legislating business, which is protected by the SEPERATION OF POWERS UNDER THE U.S. CONSTITUTION AND SERVES US WITH CITIZENS UNITED???

INSURE DOMESTIC TRANQUILITY, - we are all at odds with one another, because finally the internet has exposed the crooks involved in the Federal Reserve(who are nothing more than unnamed crooked bankers who don't even appear on the balance sheets and no one knows where the money has disappeared to!! Ben Bernanke, the Federal Reserve Bank Chairman doesn't even know where $500 BILLION DOLLARS of yours and mine hard earned taxpayer dollars disappeared to, during testimony before his cronies, the Senate Banking Committee, who instead of handcuffing and imprisoning him, slapped him on the hand and everyone said, fine and went home!! We should have WATER BOARDED BERNANKE TO FIND OUT WHERE THE,MONEY DISAPPEARED TO OVERSEAS!! Why did they let him go? Because the Federal Reserve is SELF REGULATED and set up to obey the Queen and her court of British Bankers, who are fracking you and me daily. Get it?

PROVIDE FOR THE COMMON DEFENCE – The war hawks are always beating on their drums, because through their personal investments, and INSIDER TRADING there is money to be made. The only exception is some are privileged and really believe in off shore wars, that have very little MEANING in securing FREEDOM HERE AT HOME. Those privileged like Mitt Romney are if favor of war e.g. Vietnam Conflict, but won't enlist to fight it!! COWARDS

PROMOTE THE GENERAL WELFARE – Congress will slice and dice major programs e.g. SOCIAL SECURITY, MEDICARE, MEDICAID, THE V.A. etc. while simultaneously lining their pockets with guaranteed, unwarranted huge salaries and TAXPAYER PERKS! To promote COMMON GOOD to Congress means that, WE ARE GOOD TO GO WITH THE LATEST INSIDER DEAL!

SECURE THE BLESSINGS OF LIBERTY TO OURSELVES AND OUR POSTERITY– BY NOT PROSECUTING CORRUPT BANKERS AND SHYSTERS and by attacking and dismantling its citizens, especially students, who are their own sons and daughters and arresting them for ONLY BEING GOOD PATRIOTIC CIVIC MINDED PEOPLE!!

DO ORDAIN AND ESTABLISH THIS CONSTITUTION FOR THE UNITED STATES OF AMERICA!!!!!!!!!!!!

CHAPTER 2
THE UGLY, THE BAD, THE GOOD

Question: Is the United States of America a British over seas territory? If we are not, will we ever be a British overseas territory? Will we succumb to what the Argentine Falkland Islands have become through globalization – British?

"Opponents are now moving Obama to Europe. Mitt Romney said Obama "wants to turn America into a European-style entitlement society" and "takes his inspiration from the capitals of Europe" as opposed to "the cities and small towns of America" "I want you to remember when our White House reflected the best of who we are," Romney declared, "not the worst of what Europe has become." 1

Where has Mr. Romney been all these years? Does he know that America has become a "suburb of London" and that the "Wall Street bankers" have taken a script right out of the Queen's playbook? If the Bush White House reflected the best of whom we are and Bush's treasurer, Henry Paulson, bailed the banks out and then sold us out –what great inspiration this must be for Mr. Romney- Corporate welfare, zero-2% loans, taxpayer bonus money to supposedly bankrupt bankers, CEO's, CFO's, COO's, Presidents, etc.!!

Incredibly, the Founders of the U.S. Constitution were secretive in their dealings like today's Supreme Court. James Madison initially was a "political theorist" or dreamer of a strong Federal Government. He is known as the "Father of the Constitution". He was a slaveholder who owned hundreds of Black Slaves, who cultivated cancer causing tobacco during their lifetimes. Madison quickly pushed to get the Constitution signed, sealed and delivered. He was a hypocrite. He vacillated between a strong national government and state governments. He sold us out in 1787 along with Alexander Hamilton just like G.W. Bush and Paulson did in 2008.

I wonder what James Madison was thinking when he said "before any man can be considered as a member of civil society, he must be considered as a subject of the Governor of the Universe" .2 Did he really mean before my slave becomes a member of civil society? Or, having paired up with Alexander Hamilton was he thinking about a debt slave? Or, were they both thinking longitudinally (globally) in regards to being early birds in the inner circle of a strong National Bank, espousing usury, fractional interest or "interest in perpetuity"? Or, did Madison solicit any latitude from the other 39 signers of the Constitution?

Question: Was James Madison in a Trojan horse? Were both Madison and Hamilton "war hawks"? (Since, they authored the Virginia and Kentucky Resolves which were foundational to states rights theory, that helped lead to the Civil War). Today, I wonder how many of the original aristocratic signers were actually Tories, including John Adams who was in England during the signing of the Constitution.

Question: Why have we been so heavily dependent upon giving 6% of our Federal Reserve money in guise to the Bank of England? Our Founders were power and control freaks, who had no confidence that DIRECT DEMOCRACY would work, so they concocted the elaborate and phony Electoral College scheme, that they could control through strong arm manipulation of delegates to state party conventions, which would guarantee POWER AND CONTROL over all their subjects.

The Supreme Court is like an exclusive hand picked club, whereas instead of one King, we now have "Five Kings and four queens". The Founders structured the Supreme Court majority in their favor, furthering their dominance over future serfs and continuing the principles of King George III of England. The Founders were slaveholders who got a taste of "pure" ownership of people, who they considered were nothing more than their "property".

The U.S. Constitution is an illusion of a free society. Five Supreme Court justices control the purse strings of an entire country of 330 million people! Only the U.S. Senate confirms the President's nomination of a Supreme Court justice. Why does not the full congress (House &Senate) confirm the nomination? Answer? POWER and CONTROL. Also, today these five justices are in the legislating business. They actually try to make us believe that corporations are people by legislating SUPER PACS into existence, thus pouring millions of dollars of advertisement revenue into already unbelievable wealthy T.V., radio and newspaper executives pockets.

Today, as in the year 1787 the members of Congress all seem to have dyslexia. Their brains confuse words and numbers, which to the average citizen doesn't add up to shit. Our Founders accomplished the same thing and have left us in a state of confusion. DIRECT DEMOCRACY was D.O.A. (Dead on Arrival) in 1787 and its charred remains are interred in Arlington National Cemetery along side of the "Tomb of the Unknown Soldier". In a republic which is supposed to guarantee DIRECT DEMOCRACY the Founders injected a furtherance of the ponzi scheme called the Electoral College to once again, guarantee POWER and CONTROL.

The Constitution tends to shrivel upon close examination. Question: If our Constitution is a written set of rules and laws that explain how our government is organized and how it should run, then why do we have TWO (2) sets of the same laws that are ambiguous? We have an unfair government whose purpose is totally unbalanced. The organizational parts are supposed to be separate, but those parts are interchangeable and fraudulently adaptive. Their clarity are mistakenly and knowingly misconstrued—in other words a "false belief".

CHAPTER 3
CORPORATIONS ARE PEOPLE – YEAH RIGHT!!

Our outdated constitution was supposed to be a blueprint on how the government was supposed to carry out its business. How rules were made is an understatement. The Constitution rules were made to accommodate wealthy land owners and their property interests in perpetuity. The rules conceived under such men were instituted to continue wealth and power and were selective in organization by virtue of how its members were chosen to serve.

A constitutional government is supposed to limit power......not the case in the U.S. Free wielding Congress people have unlimited access to oil terrorists, banking terrorists, and military terrorists who paint the landscape with our dead war heroes red blood in the name of uncensored greed, while simultaneously relining election coffers with "Citizens United" filthy fiat money.

I am writing this book to persist in what is right and hopefully fighting what is wrong to help make a difference to the world of our children and grandchildren. I dare to stand, think and speak on my own behalf and on behalf of others who can't.

The U.S. Department of Justice's failure to indict corrupt bankers who are continuing to commit fraud and hiding behind their corporate shield and an act of Congress (TARP) giving them practically interest free taxpayer money that was supposed to help erase toxic mortgage loans is a disgrace to the honest American people who possess integrity.

Almost four years since free bailout money was used to pay huge bonuses and things and things "have quieted down", the Justice Department (as included in the Framers powers of the President) uses the excuse "deferred prosecution" and is letting our bankers who commit fraud to police themselves like Congress has put a phony (fox guarding the hen house) office inside the Federal Reserve (which is privately held and no more than a PONZI scheme) to regulate itself!!

In 2010 at the Iowa State Fair, Mitt Romney stated, "Corporations are people" .BUT IF YOU HAPPEN TO BE BLACK LIKE THE FOUNDERS VISIONED, YOU ARE ONLY THREE FIFTHS (3/5) OF A PERSON. HOW'S THAT WORKING OUT FOR YOU FOUNDERS???? If corporations are people, then shouldn't the "people" of these incorporated banks be INDICTED FOR FRAUD? Here's an example of why America is broken: If a person goes to a 7/Eleven and steals a candy bar, that person goes to jail. However, if that person is a banker and defrauds the U.S. Government and the American people, that person gets a "keep out of jail card" and taxpayer bonus money! Many people in government still have a reckless disregard for the truth because they continue to cover up mistakes with lies, and we know this is the worst. Government works for the people, not corrupt bankers, ACCCORDING TO THE FOUNDERS!!

Our illustrious U.S. Office of the Comptroller (OCC) is totally useless in enforcing any real banking regulation e.g. mortgage backed securities, etc.

Our government leaders may have a record of academic achievement and service which has been truly exemplary, but whose personal standards and accomplishments are not models for others (especially our youth), since they don't possess high levels of integrity,, self discipline, honesty, and lack courage to do the right thing. They are in my opinion an epic failure.

We have gone from a Constitutional government to a dictatorial government. Not only are there no limits on the power of the people who run our government, but they continue to do whatever they want in the name of the U.S. Government and wrap themselves in the flag of hypocrisy, while running up huge debts for posterity. Our FOUNDING FATHERS condoned this type of behavior and etched the words " democracy" on their fallen military comrads in the name of freedom. Democracy was "coined" to subscribe to "personal greed and satisfaction or even better P.O.M.G. "peace of mind guaranteed".

Direct democracy is not only dead on arrival in America, but the people today no longer decide what laws they subscribe to. We no longer have a republican government and the people no longer hold the power of government. Our representatives no longer serve our interests and only help a few people instead of all the people. Representatives serve only their own interests.

Our Founding Fathers would lead you to believe that having representatives make the laws is more efficient, than in a direct democracy where everyone helps make the laws. Today, they would tell you making laws is time consuming business and people have to study every problem to make good and fair laws. Also, that people do not have the time, because they have to earn a living. They sell us this junk that representatives can make laws faster and better because it is their job. Yeah, right! NO. They made it a CASH COW JOB! For $175,000 PLUS . They want to keep the masses confused with ever changing directives and policies, so that they are not held accountable for their mess they create year in and year out. Business is as usual.

Our Founding Fathers lead us to believe, that "we the people" would have a say in our government and that we wouldn't give up our voice in government. BS. Do we really decide who will represent us or is it the party bosses who free handily select the "central party members in our states who always go along with the status quo and any difference of opinion by us is swept under the carpet!

Our elected representatives do not listen to the people. If you're a U.S. Senator you are safe for six (6) years! If you're a U.S. House Representative you sweat the small stuff. You need to be a sounding board to sell your crap, because you can get booted out in just two (2) years! This lower house two (2) year B.S. is to keep the people confused with all the B.S. turmoil. Remember – According to the founders, the main purpose of our republican government was suppose to promote the "common good" (what is best for the nation as a whole). Really? Ask yourself –was the free TARP MONEY doled out to the nation or only to the Wall Street B.S.'s who lied to us about being broke and nearly bankrupt due to toxic mortgage assets and then stole taxpayer money and lined their pockets with it. The founders would have you believe that people must have civic virtue to the republican government to work. True. But, they only had thoughts, not real vision to see the corruption that representatives bring to the "real" streets of America

CHAPTER 4
VAULTING ACROSS THE ATLANTIC

B ritish bankers have infiltrated the U.S. and have torn apart the very fabric of America's spirit and have pillaged the equity we had in Americas dreams and freedom. They have coerced us into thinking their superiority complex would fit tightly into their Trojan Horse! They have discounted America's wealth for unchecked meaningless sums of pity, while on the most astronomical land grab on their way to globalization of British Tyranny. They have twisted the connective social ranks of America into a meaningless hollow network of greed. They have reduced America into dust particles and have woven a fabric of pretense and plasticity unheard of since 1776.

Britain's bankers have rewritten through deregulation the very purpose and existence of the U.S. Constitution. They have vaulted across the Atlantic and have stolen the Native American spirits, which have now risen to haunt them forever!

Although somewhat philosophical, I hope this book conjures up the notion that Americans have lowered the bar towards a negative direction in their upholding the high idealism set by the Founders and hopes, the book will also help them, to hit the "RESET BUTTON" to 1776.

The War of 1812 inspired Francis Scott Key to write " The Star Spangled Banner" after soldiers at Fort Mc Henry in Baltimore raised a U.S. Flag to mark a victory over the British on September 14, 1814. At the time Americans viewed the war "as an opportunity for us to throw off Britain once and for all," said Troy Bickham, author of "The weight of Vengeance: The U.S. British Empire and the War of 1812".1

Apparently time wasn't in favor of those patriots. Their memory may have faded, but their words will never fade. We have been "Bullied to death" and cheated to death financially by Congress and need a plan to prevent this from continuing in the future. This bullying continues even after our pocketbooks are financially raped by these people. Bullying is harassment, terrorism of individualism. We the people are harassed and terrorized by these home grown "financial terrorists". If you stand by and do nothing, you are as guilty as the people stealing your money! You need to vote them out of office and start all over again!

CHAPTER 5
PROBLEMS DIRECTLY AND INDIRECTLY RELATED TO THE CONSTITUTION

Ask yourself –Are we all immigrants? Who are the Native Americans? Well folks, the Native American were the Native American Indians, Chinese and yes Mexicans. The British came well after the Italian Amerigo Vespucci visited our hemisphere and after Christopher Columbus discovered America. Even the Dutch, French, Germans and everyone else came later. So, why do we build a "Berlin Wall" on our Southern border straddling our boarder – which is a crock of B.S.? What kind of message does that send to our Mexican neighbors and all those Latin workers and their families who built Las Vegas, Los Angeles, San Francisco, Phoenix, etc. etc.?? America –wake up! The border fence is a few miles long, yet it aggravates our beautiful neighbors and pisses them off to no end, all in the name of POWER AND CONTROL! Whatever happened to that NAFTA (North American Free Trade Agreement) spirit? Remember our U.S. History lessons in school? Now days, we are pulling those old U.S. History books off our school house shelves and indoctrinating our students with new technology C.D. programs that are narrow minded, and absolutely do not address any "HOT TOPICS" for debate. These new programs provide no clues to our students about selected content and totally help shut down their THINKING processes. In other words, we are now brainwashing our children and burning our past rich history. Even the screen savers on our middle schools civics computer programs exhibit, all the queens' men carrying, not the U.S. Flag (OLD GLORY), BUT THE BRITISH FLAG past Big Ben, instead of our flag being carried by U.S. MARINES, NAVY, AIRFORCE, and ARMY PERSONNEL past the TOMB OF THE UNKNOWN SOLDIER!!!

Remember history? In 1577 Queen Elizabeth I commissioned Francis Drake to go to America and steal the gold from the Spanish living in America. She did it then, and today, the current Queen is stealing America's wealth, using the TROJAN HORSE! Lewis and Clark went up the Rivers to the north and northwest and mapped every piece of prime real estate for the Queen who ordered the slaughter of innocent NATIVE AMERICANS like CHIEF SITTING BULL, who were only trying to preserve a place in this life, God gave them. Now, our students and us must go to the internet to piece the facts together. If you are on the internet you can get these truths. But, remember in the nineteen nineties the U.S. District Court let T.V. STATIONS own newspapers and radio stations in their same MARKET

AREAS-------WHY? WHY? WHY? TO KEEP THE POWER AND CONTROL PROPAGANDA MACHINES WORKING AND SILENCE ANY FREE SPEECH!!! TO SILENCE ANY STUDENTS WHO MAY BE THINKERS AND WHO WOULD QUESTION THE VALIDITY OF THE U.S. CONSTITUTION.

[Just ask, the President of the Class of 2012 from North Haven High School (Connecticut), and a Merit Scholar. She was silenced by her own principal, from reading her own speech on graduation day, because it was too political. They taught her to THINK and now they SHUT her down. How pathetic!!] The principles of civil liberty, nondiscrimination and political freedom are at the head of not only a high school, but college education. The Constitution as written is betraying the American spirit of our schools as a center of open debate and protest by giving away the rights of its students. Instead of defending these rights, North Haven High School buckled and is stuck in draconian laws on demonstrations and policies restricting students!!

Why is it so hard to get a radio station license these days? What's really crazy about all this is that its true. Why do you think Congress doesn't want TERM LIMITS [LIKE THE President who gets just two shots at the White House or eight(8)years maximum)? The FOUNDERS didn't want the people to think about or have a mind set to upset the apple cart. The FOUNDERS HAD A KING GEORGE III MIND SET. They knew, they could control our Senate,(just like the

British House of Lords), and mirror the Queen's Court to guarantee the POWER AND CONTROL. Let the peons have their say and filibuster all day with their nonsense in the House of Representatives (just like the House of Commons, which is a meaningless venting machine for Britain's commoners (poor people) in the controlled Parliament), but we will ultimately control the actions from the Senate. ----------Were these FOUNDERS really thinking about We the People, of the people, by the people or once again were they King George III's men in a Trojan Horse?-------We the people for the King and of the people, of the King and by the people, by the King?? You be the judge—you decide…Fact or Fiction??

Something is very wrong here in America. I was born here in America, grew up here and served my country and consider myself a true patriot. Why do you sweat, year after year after year to just see these Loyalist British Bankers steal your money?? Are the people today British Loyalists or British Terrorists on the North American continent?. British Petroleum which literally screwed up the Gulf of Mexico and was slapped with a menial fine by the courts pretends now, to be our good neighbor!! It all seems to be about THEM!! Who are they?? The descendants of William The Conqueror! These people don't care about you, me or anyone else, although they will lead you to believe otherwise, through their shananagans and B.S.

I was recently on a vacation in Kauai, Hawaii and I flipped on the TV channel and there they were …….those poor bastards debating from London's House of Commons (like our House of Representatives), which is no more than the Thrones idea of a mouthpiece for the poor to vent themselves(while the House of Lords, like our Senate makes all the final decisions or has the say in what money will be spent on what and whom-----POWER AND CONTROL.

"After months of anticipation over the election date, Brown will finally play his hand, traveling to Buckingham Palace to ASK Queen Elizabeth II for permission to dissolve Parliament and call the first national vote since 2005".1 Come on Mr. Brown do you really need permission? Why not pray to William the Conqueror! Maybe he'll give you the fortitude to stand on your own two feet, instead of being a political prisoner and suppressed like Nelson Mandela was in your "Cape Town " suberb!

People envy or hate what they desire most, love and affection. Many politicians are so much in love with themselves, that they forget all about their families, who sacrificed to get them where they are. Since, the U.S. Supreme Court allowed T.V. cameras into Congress nothing has been the same. Now, we have pseudo celebrities, movie actors or Hollywood representing themselves, not you or I or anything, but Theatre for Lobbyist money and fame. Whatever happened to we the people? We were lost in sin, greed and lack of morality that these clowns don't even have a clue about. They are so engulfed in their own world that they truly represent the race of rats, lover of cats; of life's death you are guilty. They have shaved off the very fiber that our children were looking for in this short life---DECENT ROLE MODELS!! Role models, that are truthful, of high integrity and represent the best of America. Not, the sleaze bags, who steal the youth of our children, send them to some brainless war and enslave them in debts, they will never be able to afford and which will bring them disaster.

On the news, we always hear about crooks and gangs. Aren't the Republican and Democratic parties nothing more than accepted legal gangs,which continue to tear apart the very fabric of decency in people? They lie, cheat and steal (from each other, let alone including you and me) with their white collar crime B.S. so much, that people actually tend to believe some of their unadulterated B.S.!!

Think about it, the leaders of both of these so called Representative parties of WE THE PEOPLE have given us the most crooked B.S. imagined. They hood winked and blind sighted us by stealing the U.S. Treasury blind, by inducing war and war, so that the Bank of England could suck the INTEREST IN PERPETUITY from the back end of the Federal Reserve to guarantee the British monarch forever and ever. WE ARE NO MORE THAN A SUBURB OF LON-DON! GET IT?? These same politicians, many who are no more than paid thieves, steal away every value we want for our children!!

Today, private lenders are on high school, and college campuses marketing directly to students, selling them junk loans with variable interest rates and dumb credit cards with huge interest costs, which assuredly will leave students strapped in debt for years to come. Many of these loans are going to students with low credit scores! For God's sake bankers, most students have weak credit scores, because they are still in school and are STUDENTS. These low credit scores are just another scam and ponzi scheme by bankers to rape our kids pockets.

Most of our Senators are untrustworthy in my opinion. They abused their powers under the Constitution and voted for easy cash know as the TARP stimulus money, which was given to already private, rich bankers to bail them out of a false pretense that they were bankrupt. FASCISM!! What kind of B.S. is this? They literally and factually stole the U.S. Treasury blind-----WHITE COLLAR CRIME AT ITS FINEST HOUR IN AMERICAN HISTORY and the U.S. DEPARTMENT OF JUSTICE couldn't do a dam thing about it, because they are all in bed with them. Congress passed a 3 page TARP bill (act) to bailout or give our free taxpayer money to banks to give themselves bonuses!! What a crock of B.S.!! Free money with little (zero) to two (2%) percent attached, when students are paying 3 to 10 percent on their student loans!! Ask, yourself. When in hell did anyone ever hand you free money? These same tricksters have no term limits and only answer to YOUR VOTE. SO, WHAT ARE YOU WAITING FOR? GO VOTE AND STOP THEM FROM THINKING, THAT YOU ARE A MORON!!! Get rid of all these thieves!

Tea Baggers are just part of the same old gang, but with a flare for T.V. cameras. Don't be misled by their B.S. either. They are also part of the gangs. Their motto-slander, interrupt and kill off anyone who does not have allegiance to the Queen!! These people are riding Trojan horses and wait to serve the Queen anytime, anywhere, whatever the cost is to guarantee the monarchy.

Think about this-----Thousands of young military men and women were killed, since the inception of the Federal Reserve in 1913. How many of these dead human beings actually were killed in the name of FREEDOM or were they killed to perpetuate or protect the monarchy? CASH, CASH, CASH, MONEY, MONEY, MONEY to the dictator Queen. And what the hell is a constitutional monarchy? It's no more than a DICTATORSHIP with ground rule---Bring me the money and all will be well---SUCKER!!! Put the fear of God in my subjects—POLICE FORCE—and silence those who would dare question my authority to RULE THE WORLD, not just ENGLAND, BUT THE WHOLE FRACKING WORLD!!!!!!!!!! Easy cash, I'll just sit on my ass!!!

Think about this power and control tactic given to the U.S. Senate by the U.S. CONSTITUTION. The President nominates a Supreme Court Judge, but the vote for this nomination goes only to the Senate. Why not the whole Congress????-------because we want to make sure this nominee is one of ours--------POWER AND CONTROL!!! We control the Senate, we continue on the same parallel as the House of Lords in the British Parliament----keep the power, ------keep the control for the Queen!! Start the wars, borrow the cash from the PRIVATE FEDERAL RESERVE BANKERS and send SIX (6%) TO THE QUEEN VIA THE BANK OF ENGLAND, NO QUESTIONS ASKED!!!! What a FRACKING PONZI SCHEME if there ever was one and you and I let it happen. These crooks don't even need a mask to steal your money!! They just pacify the people- put a baby pacifier in there months, throw them a bone every now and then, while they steal the gold!!

CHAPTER 6
SOMETHINGS TO THINK ABOUT REGARDING THE CONSTITUTION

So, how did these unscrupulous people get into office? We let them----you and I are quilty as sin. So, what can we do to save our country from BRITISH TYRANNY (If it isn't already done)?? Vote their asses out . All of them and put some independent thinkers in government, who truly love their country. Get rid of the lobbyist money, get rid of the phony ELECTORAL COLLEGE, institute TERM LIMITS (maximum eight(8) years just like the President,, get rid of the phony FILLIBUSTER stalling B.S. tactics, get rid of LIFE TERMS and ELECT SUPREME COURT JUDGES. Allow a PEOPLES INITIATIVE into the CONSTITUTION which will help us, the people, to FREELY ELECT OUR JUDGES for a balance maximum of Eight(8) years. Get rid of the YOYO progressive income tax and institute a FLAT 15% TAX RATE. Start charging for IMPORTS to the U.S. like other foreign countries charge us to EXPORT.

TEAR DOWN THE BERLIN WALL ON OUR SOUTH BOARDER. STOP THE KILLING MACHINES in Afghanistan, Pakistan, Iraq, Syria, etc., secure our borders with our own troops and let the whole world watch us take back our country and democracy by the people. Institute a CURFEW to sweep every neighborhood in America and Drive out the forces of evil!!

Get rid of touch screen voting and vote by a standard coded paper ballot. The touch screen voting machines can be manipulated by programmers to erase your vote. We never want another FLORIDA FIASCO!! Remember, Its all about POWER AND CONROL OR WHATEVER IT TAKES AND THEY DON'T WANT YOU TO HAVE ANY.

Congress will vote themselves a fracking raise anytime they want. The raise becomes effective for Congress immediately, but you will wait 2 to 3 years before you even hear from the executive office at your company. Congress will do everything to help themselves and never to help you or your neighbor. We the people, where art thou???

We threw the fracking tea into the Boston harbor. What we didn't do was throw all the King George III loyalist's Trojan horses into the sea with a millstone hung around their necks! That was a big mistake then and it proves to be a huge mistake today. Congress has sold out

America—jobs overseas, huge government pensions to a chosen few, health insurance and health care to themselves, which they will never call SOCIALISM, because they bet Veteran.s care, Medicare and every other care you or I may never see.

CHAPTER 7
MIRROR, MIRROR ON THE WALL

The Constitution is supposed to represent every citizen., By virtually being written by fallible men, it doesn't. The porus cement which was used by the framers is like porism itself —" a proposition that uncovers the possibility of finding such conditions as to make a specific problem capable of innumerable solutions".

What the framers left out was "justice". They got the structure partially right, but forgot to add the ingredients e.g. term limits. Why? Maybe they didn't want to. Why else would they proclaim, what was discussed behind closed doors was not to be discussed for 30 years? They would most likely all be dead! Let the next or future generations deal with it! How selfish!! The framers probably would turn over in their graves if they knew how abused every citizen is today. The hurray for me and frack you attitude echoed by the leaders of Congress today is paramount only to their thinking – Our way or the highway! Or hit the road Jack and don't come back! More for us and our posterity and less for you – who cares?!?

Mirror, mirror on the wall who's the fairest of them all? The Constitution never answers that question. The Constitution is like a new born baby sucking milk from its mother. It is written in such a believable fashion, that all the good it is supposed to do is deflated once one grasps the reality, that there is no separation of powers and that all the Supreme Court justices are milking the system for life and in bed with their cousins the Senate, which only confirms them.

Did you ever wish to evade the daily routine of your life? Since, we are only on this earth for a blink of an eye lash, we need to understand how our government works in a supposedly free society. That means if you live in the good ole U.S.A. you need to understand, HOW YOU'RE BEING MASTURBATED BY THE U.S. CONSTITUTION that you are living under.

First, its "POWER & CONTROL" which is the seal of not letting go of a Senate seat, House seat, or judgeship in the name of your party, whether Republican, Democrat, Libertarian, or whatever.

Second it's the tangible and real corruption all around us, that is continually the "American Way Of Life".

Thirdly, Since there is little "reconciliation" among self serving politicians who are indirectly "FOR SALE" and bought off by "LOBBYIST tricks of the trade or MR. GREEN" (pork barrel money flows into their districts by virtually being one of the solid good old boys looking out for reelection.

Fourth, our basic willingness to take all the B.S. and actually believe things will change for the better, when in fact it only changes for the elite bankers bottom lines. You know, those that control the entire Congress!

Fifth, most people have no clue how the system works against them.

Sixth, fiat money or funny paper money is invented every day by some new policy created by those in control via their "grandiose" smoke and mirrors red tape, leaving us trillions of dollars in debt.

Seventh, Integrity, honor, respect, truthfulness, loyalty, caring, etc the Pillars of Character are not in politicians or Supreme Court justices vocabulary, since they are in bed with each other and the banking industry.

Eighth, What's good for the goose is good for the gander. There are two U.S. Constitutions. One for the bankers, supportive Congress, Supreme Court Justices (including every U.S. District Court appointee and Attorneys General and another for the average "JOE Blow" citizen, who has once again, no idea how POWER and CONTROL dictate his/her daily life. Home, home on the range has become knock, knock the sheriffs here to represent the banks interest.

Ninth, "In God We Trust" used to be a great selling "motto" in the hallowed halls of Congress. Now, it represents, the circus is in town and the actors are real with make-up, media and all the B.S. it takes to validate your "parking ticket" or the right to be the maintenance person on the banks property. All you really are doing is maintaining their property, which until you pay them the very last cent of your years of blood and sweat you don't own. It's all in your mortgage note and deed of trust, which is supposed to be filed by law with you county recorder. Oh, they have now invented a way to get around all that legally by inventing MERS (MORTGAGE ELECTRONIC REGISTRATION SYSTEM) to circumvent the laws and save on recording fees, which is being challenged in the courts today.

Tenth, Mount Rushmore's Presidents aren't looking at you any more, because their judgment days have come and gone. What remains of their legacy is all B.S. Congress's soul has been bought and sold in the name of "dough ray me".

Eleventh, Our Justice Department is now the glue that holds the "Status Quo" together. No pre-trial oral arguments allowed. Just let the judge be your jury and executioner. POWER and CONTROL OR JUST US Mentality rules baby! You're shit out of luck, let alone time! Interest money in perpetuity – We are the banking god's delight!

Twelve, New Technology is the thunder in the sky. So much corruption is now out in the open, that our government is trying to suppress its sting. Why? It is like our zoning laws – they are O.K. for the other guy, until they affect you!!

The wheels of justice grind slowly, but small. We have all heard of that declaratory sentence. But, really is this one of today's applications? Slowly maybe yes. But small-hardly

Water flows downward – The U.S. Constitution is supposed to be our barometer, thermometer, measuring stick, metric stick, etc. Then, why is it working for only a few citizens who can afford representation? There is no stop gap safeguards for freedom in today's America. Ready, aim, fire seems to be the order of the day. When in good conscience, will we ever be in a position to respect our leaders again? When will "certainty" reestablish itself in our rear view mirrors? Probably when unselfish men/women are not merely elected to fulfill sacred positions, but who themselves become examples of the values that exceed expectations of their posterity.

The U.S. Constitution is supposed to be the microcosm of democracy in action, not democracy as is to order. Today, we have super delegates deciding who should lead us to heaven. Today, DIRECT DEMOCRACY is all but a foregone conclusion as the electoral college is embedded in its core to maintain POWER AND CONTROL.

CHAPTER 8

THE SUPREME COURT – THE TEMPLE OF JUSTICE

The architecture of our elaborate Supreme Court building with its majestic columns suggests a strong republic (as mirrored by the Greeks and Romans). Democracy (also taken from Greeks) which is the cornerstone of "WE THE PEOPLE", while "In God We Trust" is an echo of the past. What happened to the WE? It has become the "We" the "Fascists". Wake up America – We is now the resurrected Nazi police state that Elie Wiesel (Night) warned us about – the faded memories of the holocaust are parallel to the fading memories of how the real American patriots, beat the oppression of the British dictator King George III.

If we continue on the present path, we will all be serfs. Once again, (if not already), we are within the serfdom of England and her connected Wall Street bankers. Terms like quantitative easing, which are no more that BOND PURCHASES is just another adjective and more B.S. protecting zero interest rates for banks to borrow more money to recharge their bottom lines and show enormous profits by the consumer borrowing rates (fractional interest –USURY) while NOT increasing the capital markets. Sixty seven (67%) percent of U.S. Senators are millionaires. Insider trading is terrific at the Capitol. Every day there is a fire sale for the lowest bidder!!

Our "Temple of Justice" the U.S. Supreme Court is supposed to be our temple of justice, not a partisan landmark of inequality. We have survived many courts that unraveled the spirit of many citizens, including the 1898 racist Supreme Court, The 2000 Republican partisan majority Supreme Court, that cared only about their selfish interest of seeing G.W. Bush becoming President and the current "Citizens United" 2010 Court.

The question is – Can we stand by and let the forces of evil work only for the corporations The Supreme Court calls, "PEOPLE" or "Real People" composing a soon to be extinct middle class?? In other words, is direct democracy a figment of our imagination or a preconceived notion of a paper over false republic run by hypocrits? Today, it seems we don't know the beginning or end of a plastic and fabricated justice system.

What were the Founding Fathers of our Constitution thinking when they created the Supreme Court of the United States of America—"JUST US".

Congress and the Supreme Court Justices only collect their pay checks, stay loose and don't get involved in the real issues of the constitution that affect themselves and modern day reality. Our courts have become a swinging door "pay as you go" cash cow for civil pass through penalties and looking past glass doors for white collar criminals e.g. bankers who only pay "civil fines" and hardly ever go to jail, e.g. robo signers who have committed forgery!

In our constitution the founders used "selective" pronouns like WE, Our, when they truly meant US, selectively. The founders believed we would truly be represented, when in fact, they left out the one thing they knew they couldn't control – How they were going to convince the people starting in 1787 to 2012.

There is no written "voting contract" when there is no election of Supreme Court Justices or term limits for justices. It takes courage to enact peoples' initiatives, which could easily place a Supreme Court nomination on each state's national ballot!! The Founders knew that would destroy their "POWER AND CONTROL" over their soon to be serfs. Congress is gutless to enact term limits for themselves or the Supreme Court Justices because they know for themselves, that they only need to serve 5 years in order to collect guaranteed pensions and health care benefits. You and I have to work 20 years plus with age guidelines to qualify for the same. The Supreme Court Justices are appointed for life!!

Henceforth, that is why the Founding Fathers enacted 6 year terms for Senators. The House of Representatives have to sweat reelection. The House of Lords (Senate) is a shoe in. Supreme Court Justices – no problem- we are sacrosanct!! (grandfathered in for a lifetime!! WOW!!

The Supreme Court Justices interpret the Constitution the way they see it as written. How do we know the validity of their own personal decisions is the correct version of interpretation? Just because they say it is so? Their cosmic interpretations sometimes are not unanimous and their majority votes are slim, leaving much doubt in the minds of the electorate. Five unelected people, sometimes become the gods of wisdom, using the Supremacy Clause, which was carved out of the figment of the Founder's imagination, as their guide to universal thinking.

The Supreme Court justices own personal idiosyncrasies, prejudices, dislikes, ethnocentrism, ideology, allegiance, loyalty, beliefs, choices, etc., all play a role in their interpretation of Constitution law. They could be further from the truth, than you think, yet closer to our redemption than we would consider right. However, they are not the only act in town and they know it. Henceforth, the sign in the hall of Congress, whose members make our laws "IN GOD WE TRUST" can be interpreted to mean " we hope we are doing the right thing".

America has lost its courage to Super Pacs, Super Gangs (Republican and Democratic national committees) and super false representatives and justices. We don't have any more time to make our democratic society withstand the confidence of all posterity. We all need to step back a notch and ask ourselves – what is really best for all of America? Not, what is best for a few demagogues. We need to get rid of the "dead" wood or "dead souls" running away from their responsibilities.

We need to once again be an "American Family", which is not afraid of our representatives or Courts, but embracing democracy from within the hallow halls of Congress, where "In God We Trust" really means responsibility, trustworthiness, caring, honesty, integrity are home here in the true American spirit of "TRUST".

Shame on all of those who violate their trust and sell trust in the name of only self interest.

We used to have more freedom to teach our children. The discontent we feel today is astonishing. We need to take pride in America. Newt Gingrich might have lost his primary campaign, but his "Contract for America" which had some teeth, might really be the answer to our problems. We all need to contract ourselves to our country's high ideals.

The "Contract" has already been signed, sealed and delivered with the blood of every U.S. Veteran, who died to make us free. We just haven't realized the "gift" it could be to all of the "good" people wailing under its flag. God Bless America.

Congress and the Supreme Court Justices have not learned the meaning of "integrity", only the meaning of words they want to hear like – pensions, life time salaries without revocation and show no remorse for those veterans who were "real" men and women, who gave their lives for their country(not for some unfair corporate,taxed, invisible, corrupt people(person) fabricated by la, la, la and brain dead individuals).Cowards die many times before their death. Valiant men die only once. My question to Congress members (who we know allowed for the stolen TARP BONUS MONEY) and Supreme Court Justices(who aren't suppose to legislate – CITIZENS UNITED)---------Are you brave enough to do the right thing for America? Have some RESPECT FOR YOUR-SELVES. If you want to be a man or woman representative or Supreme Court Justice be a real man/woman. Show your compassion for everyone, not just a few and let "In God WE Trust" take care of everything else. When was the last time you took a furlough day or a reduction is pay and gave back some time, since you only work on the average a couple of weeks out of the month, while everyone else is on the job relentlessly????????????? Unfortunately, the reality is that we will almost likely be dead and only our children will realize the "Truth" of what really mattered in 2012 and beyond.

Due to the way the Founders structured the Supreme Court there is a difference in this year's 2012 elections. The explosion of money that is showering down on candidates!! A landmark decision by the BRAIN DEAD SUPREME COURT ruling spawned the creation of Super Pac's that can accept unlimited contributions and feed the attack machines, but are not directly involved with the campaigns. Yeah right! ALL B.S. Also, there are federal political action committees (PAC'S) that are designed to help (those running for Congress, as if they need more supplemental money[remember how most of these hypocrites were against ENTITLEMENTS, but are first in line for a handout of free money like the TARP BONUS MONEY??

Millions of dollars have been received by candidates (who are for sale) in direct contributions in the current year. The richest barons in the nation are stepping forward, since the flood gates were opened to corrupt the system further with unlimited contributions, that would have been unheard of only a few years ago, say 1787!!

QUESTION? Why didn't the U.S. Supreme Court step in and reverse the lower U.S. District Court's decision to allow T.V. stations to own newspapers and radio stations in the same market, which was against the SHERMAN ANTITRUST ACT? Why didn't the Supreme Court take the initiative? Because they are also under the Five to Four guise, power and control in favor of the British mandate to control the propaganda and work the lies into truth serums! Very convenient and nice! Tell the peasants, what we want them to hear, control every major airway and keep the people down under. Allow big corporations to contribute to political campaigns, yada, yada, yada......

Moral decadence- The old saying, "the fish rots from the head on down". Our Supreme Court leaders and our Congressional leaders are rotting our nation via their own personal, selfish strategies. Some don't even hide their arrogance and racist attitudes.

CHAPTER 9
THE "ABUSE OF POWER", FASCISM, AND THE DEVIL IS IN THE DETAILS

Powers delegated under the U.S. Constitution to Congress (Paul 2 Corinthians – 8:7,9, 13-15. They should give to others in need as others give to them in their own need.

The abuse of power by Congress granting the CORPORATE WELFARE TARP – (Troubled Asset Relief Program. Public Law 110-343) money and the Supreme Courts "Silence is Golden" non interpretation of the law, is a modern day version of our Founder's secretary Alexander Hamilton's proposal in regards to establishing a "Bank of the United States" in 1790. Note the date! The seeds were already sown during the signing of the Constitution in 1787!! James Madison who was Mr. Hamilton's cohort in writing the Constitution and the Federalist papers SECRETLY supported the bank. Madison was a hypocrite. Madison wasn't just against the bank. Setting a pattern for the future, he insisted that its creation would be unconstitutional. Those who claim we can be so certain of the "original" intentions of the Founders should take note: If two of the original authors of the Constitution came to such a stark point of disagreement so quickly, what exactly does "originalism mean?"

Gordon Wood, one of the premier contemporary scholars of the founding era, while also acknowledging that they had "no special divine insight into politics" and that they were "as enmeshed in historical circumstances as we are" . Historians today can recognize the extraordinary character of the Founding Fathers. That's Mr. Wood's opinion and in my opinion I think it is full of B.S. . I guess the Founders' true spirit is really working today in light of all the Wall Street bailouts!! The Founders understood politics then as we do now-it's about making money! Quit covering up for them Mr. Wood!!! According to David Stockman of the CBO (Congressional Budget Office), "If the fed doesn't keep printing, its over"

The devil is in the details. There is a pattern, perception and concealment. The Founders actually believed that we the people weren't capable of electing Supreme Court Judges in the long run. They couldn't imagine that each state could easily put names on a ballot, use a citizen's initiative or a lottery system to elect them. They just wanted their hand picked cronies to be right where they needed them, when they needed them (e.g. 2000 Election). The result is FASCISM. Corporations are People. Elected official plus party corporate lobbyist equals FASCISM. Get the point??(1787-2012).

A cancerous lesion hid beneath a reckless disregard for the truth. The Founders vs. We the People was a great ball game, except they always come up with a winning poker hand. We the People were in the ballgame, but the Founders POWER AND CONTROL found a way to win each inning on their turf in their favor!! In the end, We the People, became once again their British serfs.

The Constitution is no more than a tax shelter for the rich and famous. It is a trial balloon consisting of FALSE HOPE for the masses. Taxes are the cancerous outgrowth of its conception. The U.S. CONSTITUTION IS DISCRIMINATORY,CONFISCATORY AND EXCLUSIONARY by its nature.

Today, a person is literally taxed out of business before he/she gets started. Today, potential small business owners are faced with taxes, fees, which are Constitutionally filtered down and literally zone businesses out of free competition. (e.g. FIFO & LIFO INVENTORY-We were first in and you are first in and first out, before you even get started). The Federal tax meter, late filing fees, etc. is always running day and night. It's no wonder businesses are moving and outsourcing to other countries. It's all bound up in the Federalist bureaucracy of paper fraud, that the Founders signed, sealed and delivered to its serfs, including the twenty-seven amendments they would have actually hoped, would have remain concealed.

Many cities, towns charge application fees (IMPACT FEES) which are ridiculously exclusionary taxes in nature, just to get started in business. Planning and Zoning Commission fees, Conservation Commission fees, Health and Safety fees(police and fire protection), Town taxes, waste disposal taxs, real estate taxes, business and personal property taxes, licenses and renewal taxes, federal, state, county, city taxes, sales taxes, (you become a tax collector for the state yourself), proprietory taxes.

Confiscatory in nature- music, copyrights. In locating a site for your business agent commission tax, title insurance tax, title company closing, commission federal tax, appraisal fee, loan origination (points) tax, business property insurance tax, business liability insurance tax, SBA TAX-(huge percentage of loan guarantee scalping fee) etc. etc. etc. etc. WE ARE TAXED TO DEATH!! Only our beloved late President Ronald Reagan's trickle down theory of INVESTMENT TAX CREDITS circumvented the Constitution and got America moving in the 1980's, even though he took away a lot of the promised Veteran's benefits.

CHAPTER 10
CITIZEN INITIATIVE

The Founders never projected any real growth estimates in the compilation of Supreme Court Justices workload. They couldn't see the alvalanche of cases coming before it. The thousands of delayed, back logged, unheard cases is surreal. The problem would have been easily fixed today if it weren't for the Founders POWER AND CONTROL B.S.

Just like there are many specialties in medicine and law, the Supreme Court could have been elected (just like the Senate), except TERM LIMITS WOULD BE IN PLACE. One four(4) year elected term. Maximum two (2) terms or eight (8) years total (just like the Presidency). States elect three (3) justices each equals one hundred and fifty justices in the pool. Justice elections are staggered so there are one hundred fifty (150 justices always seated. Specialties are sliced and diced with at least five (5) justices in thirty (30) different categories (specialties – Adult criminal law, juvenile criminal law, civil law, family law, real estate law, federal tax law, state tax law issues,, etc. etc. A three to two majority vote rules in each case. This would put cases on SPEED DIAL!!

To compensate the new court of one hundred fifty (150) judges, all the WE THE PEOPLE need to easily do: TAKE AWAY CONGRESS' AND JUDGES' PENSIONS AND HEALTH CARE BENEFITS, SINCE WITH NEW TERM LIMITS THEY WON'T NEED IT. REDUCE THEIR SALARIES BY TWENTY (20) PERCENT, GIVE THEM IMMEDIATE FURLOUGH DAYS AND CUT THEIR "SICK" DAYS IN HALF. LET THEM BUY THEIR OWN HEALTH CARE PLANS AND LET THEM OPEN THEIR OWN 401K PLANS, JUST LIKE EVERY OTHER AMERICAN AND WE'LL SEE HOW DEDICATED THEY ARE IN SERVING THEIR COUNTRY HONORABLY, SINCE IT'S A " PRIVILEDGE" TO SERVE THEIR COUNTRYMEN. THAT WILL GET THE DEAD WOOD RIGHT OUT THE DOOR AND OPEN UP OPPORTUNITIES FOR OTHER PEOPLE TO HAVE A CHANCE AT SERVING THEIR COUNTRY WITH LOYALTY AND HONOR!!! Also, each litigant would pay a flat entry fee to be determined by the court. Cases must be litigated within forty-five (45) days. FINAL ANSWER GIVEN!! NO MORE 5 TO 10 YEARS DOWN THE ROAD. This would cut down on the huge attorney and court costs and bring stability to the minds of people that justice really is a POMG (piece of mind guaranteed) in a right to a speedy trial.[take a look at how the

"In Session" of the Senate and House is scheduled. You and me work an average 40hrs a week. Congress works on average 10 days out of a month and we suckers pay each of them a salary in excess of $175,000 a year!! What a CASH COW!!! (Plus all the lobbyist money they indirectly benefit from!!!!)

The Founders purposely left out any CITIZEN INITIATIVE to be VOTED upon concerning judges. Why? When Supreme Court Judges could easily be put on the Federal Ballot via the state election VOTING BALLOT!!

Isn't there an election for the President, Senate, and House of Representatives? Who left out the Supreme Court? The Founders. Isn't this an elective government? This just didn't fall through the cracks. It is manipulation of the electorate minus the Supreme Court. IT'S CONCEALMENT AND FRAUDULENT IN NATURE BY THE FOUNDERS

By the way,. What happened to VOLUNTEERISM, that these same lawmakers vocalize from their pulpits day in and day out? Let them VOLUNTEER some of their time one day a week. That will help keep the Congressional Budget in check.

CHAPTER 11
SPECIAL CONSIDERATIONS OF THE CONSTITUTION- A SNAPSHOT

In many areas the Constitution is outdated and full of loop holes .It tends to shrivel upon closer examination. The 3/5 CLAUSE IS NOT ONLY DISCRIMINATORY, EXCLUSIONARY, BUT DOWNRIGHT CONFISCATORY IN EVERY DETAIL. The Founders actually thought that the very slaves they were fracking, were only worth 3/5 of a person.......THIS TRANSLATES INTO LESS VOTES, LESS VOTES, LESS VOTES. And the signal it sends to everyone is more POWER AND CONTROL. Let the slaves drop dead picking cotton in 100+ heat, while we are sipping our cool martinis on our shaded cool porches twiddling our umbrellas all dressed up and waiting for some action!!

The funny thing about all of this is that the racist Supreme Court has always gone along with the POWER AND CONTROL for the Queen. Howard Dean, the former governor of Vermont said it best when he said, "that the U.S. SUPREME COURT is intellectually brain dead". I agree. They have kept young people, black African Americans, women, Native American Indians and poor people down for years. It took 184 years for young people to vote. It took 178 years for Black African Americans to vote. It took 130 years for women to vote. The beat goes on and on. The 1896 Supreme Court was so racist that it allowed segregation to continue in our country for 109 years after the signing of the CONSTITUTION and for 33 years after the civil war 13th, 14th and 15th amendments were put in place.(POWER AND CONTROL FOR KING WILLIAM I MONARCHY).

RACISM is still rampant in America today. The hatred is still up front, but some Congressional members are not or will never be tried for a hate crime, because they are freely privileged to speak their minds. People want President Obama to fail and want to get his ass out of their WHITE HOUSE, BECAUSE THEY WANT ONLY BRITISH LOYALISTS in there!! Mitch McConnell would fit that mold and is another McCarthyism racist whose only job is to make Obama a one term president. The entire BLAIR HOUSE CROWD's true colors went up shortly after Obama's inauguration to send a message to the world—There is no room for a black president. By invitation only!! Congress had sent thousands of Black African Soldiers to their deaths for the Queen fighting senseless wars, while some of privilege stayed in the Virginia Beach and Newport areas, while the Vietnam war was raging or Bill Clinton, who got out of the country to study overseas, to become a Rhodes scholar and one of the Queen's men, instead of serving in the military, while my friends were being shot and killed in Vietnam or Mitt Romney who was a draft dodger and had 4 deferments and said," he was for the war in Vietnam, but would not go" ....(he must have fit in very nicely with those chanting...HELL NO, I WON'T GO!! What a COWARD!! IN MOST CIRCLES HE WOULD BE CLASSIFIED AS A DRAFT DODGER along with Dick Cheney, who also got 5 deferments, because he was convincing, that he needed his inhaler and was later hand picked to serve as Secretary of Defense with the Queen's stamp of approval.

Congress tried to impeach Bill Clinton when he was President. It didn't happen, because one man made a difference at the time. Larry Flint from Hustler magazine, had the names of 10 call girls lined up to bring down at least 10 Republican Senators, who were cheating on their wives. When Flint threatened to expose the names of the Senators, the IMPEACHMENT HEARINGS CAME TO A SCREECHING HALT!! Oh my Elizabeth what's happening today???

Have you noticed how much the Queen has lately sent her cronies to America and how much they have closed ranks lately???They have grabbed prime T.V. commentator jobs. Why not? She and her cronies control the media,, but holy cow what's this thing called the WORLD WIDE WEB?? How can we control that? OH, OH, OH, The PONZI Schemes are getting out of the bag. How the frack can we control the Freedom of Speech NOW??

History has it, that in 1431 during the Hundred Year War, the lovely French woman Joan of Arc was tied to a stake, with her hands behind her back and burnt to a crisp by the Pro-British Bishop to silence her. Could that happen in America? YOU BET. It is happening EVERY DAY!!

CHAPTER 12
FREEDOM OF EXPRESSION

Ask yourself – Should freedom of expression ever be cut short? It seems to be based upon how much money you got or who you know in the political arena. Let's examine two (2) similar cases in which the U.S. Supreme Court found one person guilty and never had the opportunity, due to a lack of judgment, to hear a potential second parallel case. The high court found Irvin Feiner guilty and he went to prison. Feiner appealed the decision and said that the police were trying to silence his views in violation of his right to freedom of speech. Here we go!

Irving Feiner vs. New York 1951. "On the evening of March 8, 1951 college student Irving Feiner stood on a wooden box on a street corner in Syracuse, New York. He was addressing a racially mixed crowd of about seventy-five people. The police received a telephone call about the meeting, and two police officers were sent to find out what was happening.

Feiner urged the African Americans in the crowd to take up arms and fight for equal rights. He urged them to attend a meeting later that night to talk about equal rights. Feiner told the crowd that the president of the United States, the mayor of the city, and other public officials were bums. His words gave the impression that he was trying to get the people to become violent and to fight for their rights.

The crowd became restless. Feelings both for and against the speaker were rising. For thirty minutes, the police made no effort to interfere with the speech, but they were concerned about the crowd. There was some pushing and shoving, and as Feiner continued to speak, one man threatened him with violence.

The officers asked Feiner three times to get off the box. Then they demanded that Feiner stop talking. Finally, the officers arrested Feiner and charged him with disorderly conduct. This law makes it a crime to encourage people to use violence. The officers said that they had acted to control the crowd, to keep the peace, and to prevent injury.

At his trial, the state court found Feiner guilty and sentenced him to prison. Feiner appealed the decision. Feiner said that the police were trying to silence his views in violation of his right to freedom of speech.

Do you think Feiner's speech was a lawful speech? "Did it go beyond persuasion, and did he try to encourage a riot? Did the police violate Feiner's right of free speech?

Opinion 1: The police did not violate Feiner's right of free speech.

The officers making the arrest were responsible for keeping law and order. They were not trying to keep Feiner from expressing his views and opinions. The way Feiner acted and the immediate danger of the audience becoming violent were reasons enough for the police to arrest him. Freedom of speech does not include the right to try to make people use violence or to riot.

Opinion 2: The police did violate Feiner's right of free speech.

The facts do not show any immediate danger of a riot or disorder. It is not unusual that some people at public street meetings push, shove, or disagree with the speaker. The police had a duty to protect Feiner's right to speak. The crowd was restless, but the police did not try to quiet it. One man threatened Feiner, but the officers did nothing to discourage this man. Instead, the police acted only to stop Feiner's speech."1

NOW, lets fast forward a similar example to 2008, when Sarah Palin called presidential candidate Barack Obama a terrorist and a man from her crowd said, " We should kill him!"

Palin's words gave the impression that SHE was trying to get the people to become violent and to fight for their rights!! The crowd became restless. For 30 minutes, the police made no effort to interfere with her speech, but they were concerned about the crowd As Palin continued to speak, "one man threatened to kill Barack Obama with violence".2

The officers in Carson California, nor Englewood, Colorado where she repeated herself, never asked Palin three times to get down from the podium she was speaking from. The officers never demanded that Palin stop talking. Finally, the officers NEVER ARRESTED SARAH PALIN, nor did they ever charge her (WHICH THEY SHOULD HAVE) with disorderly conduct. This law makes it a crime to ENCOURAGE people to use violence. The officers contend they acted to control the crowd, kept peace and prevented injury.

Palin never went to court. She was never tried for disorderly conduct or INCITING A RIOT and never sentenced to prison. WHY???

Did Palin's speech go beyond persuasion and did she try to encourage a RIOT? Sarah Palin's speech gave the impression that she was trying to get the people to become violent and to fight for their rights. The way Palin acted and the immediate danger of the audience becoming violent were REASONS ENOUGH for the police to ARREST PALIN. THEY NEVER DID ARREST HER!!WHY? WHY?

She was a privileged former governor and possible Vice Presidential candidate. She was a candidate for one of the highest,, honorable offices in the U.S. and everyone looked the other way!! One man threatened to kill Barack Obama and the officers did nothing to discourage this man. Why? The FOUNDERS knew all about POWER AND CONTROL and how a police force would protect the PRAETORIAN CLASS from all opposition.

"Some people in the American colonies had suffered- and in some cases died- for expressing their ideas. Three examples are Mary Dyer, John Buckner, and John Peter Zenger.

Mary Dyer lived in Massachusetts. In 1660, the Puritan leaders had her put to death. The Puritans said that she taught people that slavery, war, and the death penalty were wrong.

John Buckner was a printer in Virginia. In 1682, he used his press to print the laws of the colony. The governor of Virginia said that Buckner did not have permission to print the laws. He banned all printing presses in the colony. The governor said, "Printing has encouraged [the people] to learn and even criticize the best government. God, keep us from free schools and printing".

John Peter Zenger was a newspaperman in New York. In 1735, he wrote an article saying that the government was dishonest. The governor had Zenger arrested and thrown in jail. After a long trial, the court set Zenger free. The jury decided that what Zenger had said was true. These are some reasons why the Founders and others believed it was necessary to protect freedom of expression. It is why they insisted that this protection be in the Constitution."3

SO WHAT HAPPED TO THAT EXPRESSION? JUST ASK THE OCCUPY WALL STREET PROTESTORS.

Today, Thank God for the Alex Joneses, Ed Schultzes, Keith Obermmans, Dylan Ratigans, Karl Dennigers, Sarah Huffingtons, William Blacks, Market Tickers, Capitol Watchers, Gerald Celentes, Matt Tiabbis, Mandelmanns, and Max Kaiser's and Jonathan Turleys of this world who are true patriots and bring the TRUTH (whether people want to hear it or not) to the American public. These honorable people OFFSET and far outweigh the B.S. rendered by the O'reillys, Becks, Hannitys, and Limbaugh's of the world.

Interesting- Two sets of opinions. e.g. two sets of the CONSTITUTION. One for me and one for you! How diddle squat nice!!! All wrapped up in the flag, all wrapped up in fine print for every poor credit card holder to beware of the 25-30% interest rate we are screwing you for!!

CHAPTER 13
FREEDOM OF SPEECH FROM THE FCC WITH LOVE

"About 10 years ago, the Federal Communications Commission began a trend of deregulation that changed the face of radio broadcasting in the U.S. (What took them so long? POWER AND CONTROL! Medium and small market broadcast owners were being purchased left and right by larger broadcasters, at prices they couldn't refuse! Also, deregulation allowed larger owners to purchase other large media companies to form massive broadcast conglomerates...which put more little guys out of business. Today, the radio industry has a new face. Community groups from around the country rose to show their anger at the FCC for such changes, which eventually silenced many voices in cities across America. So, the government looked into the concept of Low-Power broadcasting (LP) which includes television, and radio outlets. There was various criteria for being eligible [TO KEEP THE COMPETITION OFF THE MARKET AND SILENCE THEM] mainly for non-profit, and public service groups. This keeps the POLITICAL NON-SENSE IN AND THE VOICE OF WE THE PEOPLE AT BAY!!

Only SELECT IDEAS OR PROPAGANDA ARE ALLOWED ON THE 'BIG OLE BOYS NETWORKS", to guarantee wealthy T.V. and radio owners are in the pockets of politicians,, who run their advertisements through donated other peoples cash(OPM) money!!

The FCC's position concerning T.V. and radio is a classic example of CONTROLLING the VOICE OF THE PEO-PLE .Where is the protection in the CONSTITUTION for the people's voice?? IN THE TOLIET!

Their Low-Power (LP) means FEW LISTENERS---DON'T WORRY – WE STILL ARE FRAGMENTALY DESTROYING THE PEOPLE'S VOICE IN AMERICA!!

There was various criteria for being eligible (for low Power (LP) T.V. and radio) mainly for non-profit and public service groups (BIG BROTHER IS WATCHING YOU MEN-TALLY).

Many applicants must be SCREENED AND CHOSEN for assigned frequencies, which are available in their area and MUST broadcast via LOW POWER COVERAGE [TO KEEP YOUR VOICE OUT OF THE MARKETPLACE]"

The Supreme Court on 6/21/2012 UNANIMOUSLY threw out fines and other penalties against broadcast companies that violated the Federal Communications Commission policy regulating curse words and nudity on television airwaves. All of this reflects PROTECTING THE COURT

PROTECTING THEIR FRIENDS, WHO ARE ON THE RECEIVING END OF MULTI MILLION DOLLAR POLITICAL SUPER PAC FUNDS. OTHERWORDS THEY ARE BEING REWARDED ALSO BY THE CITIZENS UNITED PASS THROUGH!!!!!!"1

The owners of these mega television stations are already pathetically wealthy and will continue to reap the harvest, while not spending a single dime on civil penalties. So, what good (WHERE IS FOR THE COMMON GOOD …IN THE CONSTITUTION?) is the FCC and the U.S SUPREME COURT??? ……….POWER AND CONTROL!!! Congress and Banksters, just let NO REGULATION continue to feed the heirs at the trough of "NO RETURN TO CITIZENS!".

MEANWHILE, OCCUPY WALL STREET PROTESTERS ARE STRIPPED, BEATEN WITH A BATON (DILL DOW) AND NAKEDLY DEPRIVED OF THEIR RIGHTS TO ASSEMBLY!!

The FOUNDERS knew all about POWER AND CONTROL and how a police force would protect the PRAETORIAN CLASS from all opposition.

"Some people in the American colonies had suffered- and in some cases died- for expressing their ideas. Three examples are Mary Dyer, John Buckner, and John Peter Zenger.

Mary Dyer lived in Massachusetts. In 1660, the Puritan leaders had her put to death. The Puritans said that she taught people that slavery, war, and the death penalty were wrong.

John Buckner was a printer in Virginia. In 1682, he used his press to print the laws of the colony. The governor of Virginia said that Buckner did not have permission to print the laws. He banned all printing presses in the colony. The governor said, "Printing has encouraged [the people] to learn and even criticize the best government. God, keep us from free schools and printing".

John Peter Zenger was a newspaperman in New York. In 1735, he wrote an article saying that the government was dishonest. The governor had Zenger arrested and thrown in jail. After a long trial, the court set Zenger free. The jury decided that what Zenger had said was true. These are some reasons why the Founders and others believed it was necessary to protect freedom of expression. It is why they insisted that this protection be in the Constitution."3

SO WHAT HAPPED TO THAT EXPRESSION? JUST ASK THE OCCUPY WALL STREET PROTESTORS.

Today, Thank God for the Alex Joneses, Ed Schultzes, Keith Obermmans, Dylan Ratigans, Karl Dennigers, Sarah Huffingtons, William Blacks, Market Tickers, Capitol Watchers, Gerald Celentes, Matt Tiabbis, Mandelmanns, and Max Kaiser's and Jonathan Turleys of this world who are true patriots and bring the TRUTH (whether people want to hear it or not) to the American public. These honorable people OFFSET and far outweigh the B.S. rendered by the O'reillys, Becks, Hannitys, and Limbaugh's of the world.

Interesting- Two sets of opinions. e.g. two sets of the CONSTITUTION. One for me and one for you! How diddle squat nice!!! All wrapped up in the flag, all wrapped up in fine print for every poor credit card holder to beware of the 25-30% interest rate we are screwing you for!!

CHAPTER 14

THE SUPREME COURT TO THE PEOPLE OF MONTANA —GO TO HELL, YOU'RE SHIT OUT OF LUCK!

C ourt's ruling reaffirms CITIZENS UNITED DECISION " A narrowly divided Supreme Court on 6/25/2012 reaffirmed its landmark 2010 decision allowing corporations to spend unlimited money on elections, deciding five to four(5/4 right down POLITICAL PARTY LINES, JUST LIKE THE BUSH/GORE VOTE) that a STATE COURT was wrong to uphold Montana's century-old ban on political spending by businesses.

The decision –TWO PARAGRAPHS ISSUED WITHOUT HEARINGS OR DEBATE –further inflamed an argument over the role of big money in politics, which has become a central feature of the expensive race for the White House between President Barack Obama and Mitt Romney. A constellation of independent groups is poised to spend $1 billion or more on the 2012 elections, much of it raised in SECRET from billionairs and corporations. The spending is made possible in part by the court's 2010 decision in Citizens United v. Federal Election Commission, which found that companies and unions have a free-speech right to donate unlimited amounts for and against candidates."1

[In essence, the Supreme Court is telling us that CORPORATIONS ARE PEOPLE!! Think about this-REVERSE MORTGAGES—REVERSE CORPORATIONS ARE PEOPLE – PEOPLE ARE CORPORATIONS THROWS A WRENCH INTO ALL THEIR CAPTIVE REASONING CALLED 'TAX BREAKS".]

The case involved a Montana law forbidding corporate political spending. The law dated to 1912, when the "copper kings" and other mining barons controlled the state's politics. Montana's high court said that, even after Citizens United, the legacy of CORRUPTION AND OTHER FACTORS UNIQUE TO MONTANA JUSTIFIED A BAN ON SPENDING BY CORPORATIONS REGULATED BY THE STATE".2

SHAME ON THE U.S. SUPREME COURT!! Their decision solidifies the FOUNDERS realm of thinking POWER AND CONTROL!! ......FASCISM WITH ALL ITS TRIMMINGS!! THE COMMON GOOD IS LOST IN THE FABRIC OF THE RINGING CASH REGISTERS OF "FINDER'S FEES, KICKBACKS, CAMPAIGN DONATIONS AND LOBBYIST ETERNAL INFLUENCE AND CONTROL".

THE U.S. SUPREME COURT HAS SOLD AMERICA'S SOUL TO THE DEVIL!

CHAPTER 15
WILLIAM E. GLADSTONE 1809-1898

Here is a synopsis from Gladstone-
" Show me the MANNER in which a nation cares for its dead and I will measure with mathematical exactness the tender mercies of its people, their respect for the laws of the land, and their loyalty to high ideals".

"Justice delayed is justice denied"

"WE LOOK FORWARD TO THE TIME WHEN POWER TO LOVE WILL REPLACE THE LOVE OF POWER. THEN WILL OUR WORLD KNOW THE BLESSINGS OF PEACE".1

Now, let's take a look to see if Americans respect the law of the U.S. CONSTITUTION, the laws of America:

"The Dover Air Force Base mortuary for years disposed of parts of troops remains by cremating them and dumping the ashes in a Virginia landfill, a practice that officials have since stopped in favor of burial at sea.

The Dover mortuary, the main point of entry for America's war dead and the target of federal investigations for possible mishandling of remains, engaged in the practice from 2003 to 2008, Air Force officials said. The MANNER of disposal was not disclosed to relatives of fallen service members.

Air Force officials acknowledged the practice. They said the procedure was limited to fragment or portions of body parts that were unable to be identified at first or were later recovered from the battlefield, and which family members had said could be disposed of by the military.

Lt. Gen. Darrel Jones, the Air Force's deputy chief for personnel, said the body parts were first cremated, then incinerated and then taken to a LANDFILL by a military contractor. He likened the procedure to the disposal of medical waste.

Jones could not estimate how many body parts were handled in that way. "That was the common practice at the time, and since then, our practices have improved," he said.

Gari-Lynn Smth, portions of whose husband's remains were disposed of in the landfill after his 2006 death in Iraq, said she was" appalled and disgusted" by the way the Air Force had acted. She learned of the landfill burial earlier this spring in a letter from an official at the Dover mortuary.

"My only peace of mind in losing my husband was that he was taken to Dover and that he was handled with dignity, love, respect and honor," Smith said. "That was completely shattered for me when I was told that he was thrown in the TRASH,"

An Air Force document shows that the landfill is in KING GEORGE COUNTY, VA. Officials with Waste Management, which operates the landfill, said the company was not told about the origin of the ashes.

"We were not specifically made aware of that process by the Air Force," said Lisa Kardell, a spokeswoman for the company.

The mortuary changed it policy in June 2008, Jones said. Since then, the Navy has placed the cremated remains of body parts in urns that are buried at sea.

THE AIR FORCE ACKNOWLEDGED THAT THE MORTUARY HAD LOST A DEAD SOLDIER'S ANKLE AND AN UNIDENTIFIED BODY PART RECOVERED FROM AN AIR CRASH, HAD SAWED OFF A MARINE'S ARM SO HIS BODY WOULD FIT IN HIS CASKET, AND HAD IMPROPERLY STORED AND TRACKED OTHER REMAINS."2

CHAPTER 16
WHAT AND WHO THE CONSTITUTION PROTECTS

The Constitution protects Banks, which were the HOLY GRAIL OF THE FOUNDERS innermost thoughts when they formulated our new nation. Why? Because through Power and Control the dream and CASH COW lives on forever!! Sure, we have survived for 236 years, but who have been the benefactors of all the sweat, sacrifice and tears? You guessed ....THE BANKSTERS!!

Let's take a look at some of the modern day ploys used in banking.

Primary Mortgage Insurance, better known as PMI is automatically included in and collected from your mortgage payment monthly, if you put down less than 20% on your home. If you default the banks still get their money no matter what, and the buyer pays insurance to protect the banks! Any bank balances due, are also written off on the Banks 1099 corporate tax forms even though you are stuck paying the capital gains tax to the government on the difference! The bank probably insured your life, just like your corporate boss and you probably never knew it!

One of the biggest banking scams besides the TARP bailout is that banks even come out of a short sale of your home, smelling like a rose. Example: A $150,000 loan is recovered even if it is put on the market and sells for only $75,000. Even if it loses it value say to $75,000 and is upside down. These bankers are no more than scam artists.

Banks are home grown "DOMESTIC TERRORISTS". They insult you, threaten you through their attorneys and eventually foreclose on you when you are out of work, especially if their LIAR LOANS AND SUBPRIME INTEREST SCAMS didn't work out in their favor. THEIR BANKING VISION PLAN AND MOTTO IS WE OWN YOU! As long as you have a mortgage and they are cleaning up on your hard earned interest payments............you are nothing more to them, than a maintenance person, for their property until you pay them, that last copper penny of interest and principle they suck out of you. They own you and as one banker put it, " If you fail to pay us back. We will come after you and you will be living in a TENT".

So, why did we give banks the bail out money and why are we bailing out private entities? Since, when did government crawl in bed with corporations, AND RAISE THE FASCIST FLAG? When our FOUNDING FATHERS let them! Our FOUNDING FATHERS were shrewd businessmen! They just LEFT ALL OF THE BANKING FRILLS OUT OF THE CONSTITUTION!!!

Insurance companies, banks, and credit card companies are all huge government lobbyist cash cows with no strings attached. What ever happened to "integrity"? Now, the U.S. Supreme Court thinks that they are voters (people). To Big to fail-this is unadulterated B.S. They milked us for almost zero percent loans, which they turned into billions in profits in just 3 years! Hell, if someone gave you almost free money, you could turn that into a nifty profit.

These entities can now give unlimited amounts of cash to help get their man /woman elected. Show us the money! No questions asked. Where the frack is WE THE PEOPLE in all this? You and me don't exist in their scheme of crooked things!! And where is the Department of Justice in all of this to help protect us against this openly wide spread white collar crime game? No where to be found. The Department of Justice says they only enforce what Congress deems as a law. Notice—what Congress passes as law! The TARP money is very nicely gift wrapped, no STRINGS ATTACHED to banks, practically interest free and TARP is the law! WHAT A CIRCLE JERK!! How convenient! They really think you and I are really stupid! And guess what? WE ARE STUPID FOR TAKING ALL THIS B.S. and letting them get away with it day after day. SILENCE IS GOLDEN TO THEM! They know all the hoopla and decent will die down with time and they can always blame it on the other guy!

Big oil companies are nothing more than "domestic and foreign terrorists". They get unbelievable corporate welfare tax breaks from Congress and they hit, run and hide. They raise the price on you at the gas pump for awhile------people complain-----they lower the price and hide from you until summer vacations or whatever, and again shoot the price back up. They make billions and billions for doing nothing more than using capitalism as their guise.

Exxon screwed up the coast of Alaska, was taken to court and fined billions of dollars for awhile, until time passed and another Federal Judge came on the scene and reduced the original jury award almost in half!!! The judge is Constitution protected by appointment and insulated!!

BRITISH PETROLEUM (BP) really fracked up the Gulf of Mexico, killing our wildlife and beautiful marshlands and got a slap on the wrist for it and minimum fines. Now, they run ads on television brought to you by B.P. and all of us who call the Gulf Home. How thoughtful and how nice! The British have actually moved into the Gulf area and call them- selves NEIGHBORS!! BUYER, BEWARE!! THEY ARE HERE TO FRACKING STEAL YOUR COUNTRY!! WAKE UP AMERICA!!

That pipeline the oil industry wants to build from north to south through America is stuck in gear, only because the oil companies want to redraw the lines of demarcation, so they don't have to pay the EXPORT/IMPORT TAXES(because they will be marketing it to foreign interests and right back to us). Yet, they will take all the TAX CREDITS imaginable under CONSTITUTIONAL LAW!!

The Constitution also protects Congress people, who will never set TERM LIMITS for themselves. We need to find out which Senators and House members have already served 8 years and target them and vote their asses out of Congress. They are DEAD WOOD and only serve their OWN needs and wants. We must stop the insider trading horseplay. It takes less than one year to train an already qualified person about the inner workings or the ropes of how to legislate on Capitol Hill.

We need to change the MINDSET of Congress with a more progressive approach to streamline and SIMPLIFY LANGUAGE in bills passed by Congress, by STOPPING THE COMBINING OF BILLS and trying to trailer them!!

WE NEED ONE BILL, ONE ITEM, SIMPLIFIED AND PUT IN PLAIN ENGLISH FOR THE VOTERS. Something streamlined like the new CONSUMER PROTECTION TRUTH IN LENDING breakdown law, which spells out in short language, WHO, WHAT, WHEN, WHERE, WHY AND HOW!

REMEMBER, these Congress people are hell bent on staying in Congress forever to maintain their egos, cash cow of insider trading, using the public's time to make personal business deals and to maintain POWER AND CONTROL.

Today, while most Americans are trimming their budgets to the bone, Senators and House members CONTINUE to take FACT FINDING TRIPS AROUND THE WORLD! In essence, they take their wives and family on a VACATION ON THE TAXPAYER'S DIME, when you can't afford to fill your own gas tank up to go to work and earn the money to PAY FOR THEIR TRIP!! WAKE UP AMERICA, YOU ARE BEING FLEECED OUT OF YOUR WALLET AND PLAYED FOR A SUCKER!!

When a country loses controls due to LOPSIDED CONSTITUTIONAL AUTHORITY like America has of lately, YOU HAVE A RUNAWAY FASCIST CORPORATE WELFARE STATE, THAT WE ARE EXPERIENCING IN AMERICA TODAY! VERY LITTLE DIRECTION WITH A LOT OF POMP AND CEREMONY!

IT IS NOT WRITTEN ANYWHERE THAT LIFE IS FAIR-----WE MAKE IT UNFAIR BY BEING PASSIVE!!

The youth of America and the new PROGRESSIVES like the admired Ron Paul activists, who step up to the plate and get involved with the mechanics of their country's governing powers are better off for it! People in general need to STOP WHINING AND COMPLAINING and get involved, and take an interest in what is happening to THEM! Only then will America begin to dig its way out of DEBT and make fair changes for everyone.

THE CONGRESS AND CONSTITUTION ALSO PROTECT THE TAX MAN.

When Paul Revere warned us that the British were coming, he was instructed to hang a lantern-ONE IF BY LAND, TWO IF BY SEA!

Our country has become a CARRY OVER of the same old tricks exercised by King George III's TAX COLLECTION SCHEMES.

A friend of mine, now deceased, was an excellent capitalist. He was dedicated, loyal, trustworthy, honest, caring person who lived a life of honor and high integrity. He was a Funeral Director, who worked very hard, built and operated a family owned business. He said to me, "my biggest fear of losing the business and all my hard work, would be my inability to pay my business property TAXES". He collected and saved all of his Social Security checks and put them in his desk drawer. He would then wait until December of every year and cash all of the current years 12 checks AND GO PAY THE TAX COLLECTOR. He did this year after year and worked in his practice in retirement to alleviate his fear of taxes and the burden they might place on his family!

Taxes are CUMULATIVE, but necessary. They pay the merry –go- round of expenses to run our government. However, come on, you buy a car and its taxed year after year. Within ten years, you have paid for the car TWICE! Go look at all of your house bills and high light all of the taxes you pay and you will probably throw up.

AMBASSADORSHIP APPOINTMENTS are no more than "Payola" for voting on and signing for the necessary control of power to stay in place. e.g. the Secretary of State, Florida. The Secretary of State was given an ambassador job to Chad for signing off early on George Bush's presidency win vote, before the people of Florida had a chance to complete the voting process. Her early bird write off, undoubtedly played a pivotal role in the T.V. stations influencing the west and west coast voting, EVEN THOUGH AL GORE WON THE POPULAR VOTE. Her reward, a cushy, well paying, B.S., bloated, government cash cow job!! ONLY IN AMERICA AND PROTECTED BY THE CONSTITUTION AND THE ELECTORAL COLLEGE!!

CHAPTER 17

DOES THE CONSTITUTION LIMIT THE POWERS OF GOVERNMENT??

Did the Framers of our government really want to limit the powers of our government? Did they really want to be sure that no one group of people in government would have too much power? You can be sure the separation of powers and checks and balances is a fairy tale.

The Legislative branch, which includes both the Senate and the House of Representatives was given the power to make laws we live under. Let's examine some of the "Bugs" in the Powers Delegated to Congress.

Under Article I Section 8 #3 It tells us Congress shall have the Power to borrow Money on the credit of the United States.

But, from whom? Until 1913 it was a free for all. After that, it got worse, when President Woodrow Wilson, the Financial reformer, in collusion with his cronies, helped create the "Federal Reserve Act on 12/23/1913". Notice the date!! It was 2 days before Christmas, when nobody was thinking about anything, but the holiday, when they railroaded the most destructive legislation in U.S. History!! This opened the floodgates for the U.S. to borrow back its OWN MONEY deposited with the Federal Reserve Bank, which became the SERVICER OF TAXPAYER FEDERAL INCOME TAX DEPOSITS!! WE HAVE TO PAY INTEREST TO A PRIVATE BANK TO BORROW OUR OWN FRACKING MONEY JUST BECAUSE THEY ARE SAFEGUARDING IT !!!!!!!!!!!!!!The Founders knew the people during their time were against establishing a Federal Bank having been enraged how King George III of England " taxed them to death. TODAY, TO BIG TO FAIL BANKS LIKE BANK OF AMERICA ARE AGENTS FOR THE INTERNAL REVENUE SERVICE (IRS). BANK OF AMERICA, CLAIMING THEY WERE BROKE WAS BAILED OUT WITH TAXPAYER STIMULUS MONEY!! HOW PATHETIC!!

In the 1920's The Bank of England persisted and saw an opportunity on the open market speculation of making a ton of "easy money" by cashing in on Wilson's deal!

Under Article I Section 8 #5 The Congress shall have Power to coin Money, regulate the Value thereof, and of foreign Coin, and fix the Standard of Weights and Measures. IT DOESN'T SAY CONGRESS HAS THE POWER TO PRINT PAPER FIAT MONEY!!

The Founders left out FIAT PAPER MONEY!! They never dreamed the PRINTING PRESSES WOULD BE WORKING OVERTIME PRINTING USELESS UNSE-

CURED DEBT. The Banking Act of 1933 created the FDIC, the U.S. Banking Holding Companies. Franklin D. Roosevelt ended all gold and silver certificates (the metallic standard). This led to the passage of the Banking Act in 1935, NOW GET THIS, WHICH SET MEMBER TERMS AT 14 YEARS!!(POWER AND CONTROL). This created maximum employment, more IRS dollars and the guise that the Feds were regulating "BANK HOLDING COMPANIES". They weren't regulating them, they were POINTING US IN THE DIRECTION OF FASCISM.

THE CONSTITUTION AND ITS RULES ARE LIKE ZONING LAWS------THEY ARE O.K. FOR THE OTHER GUY, UNTIL THEY AFFECT YOU!!!!!!! OUR FOUNDERS ZONED OUT THE BANKING MODEL KNOWING DAMN WELL THEY COULD CIRCUM-VENT THE ISSUE BY SECTION 8 #18!!

Under Article I Section 8 #18. To make all Laws which shall be necessary and proper for carrying into Execution the foregoing Powers, and all OTHER POWERS vested by this Constitution in the Government of the United States, OR IN ANY DEPARTMENT OR OFFICER THEREOF.

Henceforth, the Constitution is not a static document and continues to move towards DEREGULATION depending upon who is in POWER AND CONTROL!!

Fast forward to 6/26/12: The telltale sign of corrupt law-makers was raised even higher by the INSIDER TRADING behind the hallow halls of Congress. Read on

"Breaking from Newsmax.com: 34 CONGRESSMEN ALTERED PORTFOLIOS AFTER TALKS WITH FED OFFICIALS. AS THE AMERICN ECONOMY WAS CRATERING IN THE WANING DAYS OF THE BUSH ADMINISTRATION, TOP LAWMAKERS WERE TALKING WITH THE TREASURY SECRETARY AND THE CHAIRMAN OF THE FEDERAL RESERVE AND THEN REMAKING THEIR OWN PERSONAL FINANCIAL PORTFOLIOS"

NOW, This is exactly what the Founders let happen, They created a "LOOP HOLE" TO ALLOW A FEDERAL BANK TO COME INTO EXISTENCE AND PROMOTE CORRUPTION!

NOW, Let's take a peek at the Powers Denied to Congress

Under Article I Section 9 #7 No money shall be drawn from the Treasury, but in Consequence of Appropriations made by Law:

How nice. Once again, Let us fast forward from 1787 to 2008. Congress quickly passes the TARP STIMULUS BILL (which in my opinion, turns out to be a legal CASH COW money laundering ponzi scheme in favor of liar banks to big to fail. WHY DIDN'T CONGRESS JUST TELL THE BANKS TO START SELLING OFF THEIR TAGH MAHAL MEGA WHITE ELEPHANT ASSETS LIKE EVERY OTHER CHAPTER 11 BUSINESS IN AMERICA? WHY DIDN'T CONGRESS JUST NATIONALIZE THE BANKS? WHY DIDN'T CONGRESS BREAK UP THE MEGA BANKS INTO SMALLER MANAGE-

ABLE BANKS? WHY DID THEY JUST HAND THEM THE FRACKING MONEY?

THE ANSWER TO ALL OF THE ABOVE QUESTIONS------- BECAUSE INTERSTATE BANKING IS BASELESS. THEY OPERATE FROM NEVER, NEVER LAND e.g. THE BANK OF ENGLAND AND ALL HER TRIBUTARIES THROUGH OUT THE BRITISH KINGDOM!!

WOULD THE NATIONALIZATION OF THE BANKS CREATE AN ILLUSION OF SOCIALISM? YES

HOWEVER, THE BANKS TOOK CORPORATE WELFARE MONEY UNDER THE TARP PROGRAM!!

Under Article I Section 9 #8 No title of Nobility shall be granted by the United States: And no Person holding any Office of Profit or Trust under them, shall, without the Consent of Congress, accept of any present, Emolument, Office, or Title, of any kind whatever from any King Prince, or foreign State.

The FOUNDERS threw this into the CONSTITUTION TO OFFSET THE PEOPLES DISREGARD FOR KING GEORGEiii, BUT THEY REALLY KNEW HOW TO MANIPULATE THE MASSES THINKING BY RIDING THE TORY TROJAN HORSE. FRACK THE WIG, WE'LL JUST CUT OUR HAIR SHORTER. THE PEOPLE WILL NEVER RECOGNIZE US! AND THE PEOPLE BOUGHT IT, LINE,HOOK AND SINKER!!!!

THINK ABOUT IT. OUR PRESIDENTS BOW TO THE QUEEN. DID YOU EVER SEE THE QUEEN BOW

OR CURTSY TO ONE SINGLE U.S. PRESIDENT? NO AND SHE NEVER WILL. WHY? BECAUSE SHE HAS THE POWER AND CONTROL OVER HIM. SHE SEES HIM AS A RENTER OF HER PROPERTY IN THE WORLD VISION OF WILLIAM THE CONQUEROR!!

OUR PRESIDENTS ACCEPT PRESENTS AND EXCHANGE GIFTS WITH FOREIGN DIGNITAR-IES. (BEWARE OF THE GIFTS IN ONE HAND AND THE INIQUITIES IN THE OTHER HAND! REMEM-BER THE CONSTITUTION!!)

Under Article I Section 8 #11 Power to declare war – so we need money to finance wars. So where do we get it from? The Federal Reserve (our own income tax money sent over by the treasury for safekeeping) which is a GSE (GOV-ERNMENT SPONSERED ENTERPRISE). WHICH MEANS TOTAL FASCISM. WE'RE IN BED WITH SECRETIVE PRIVATE BANKERS, WHO CHARGE US INTEREST ON OUR OWN FRACKING MONEY?

Under Article I Section 8 #15 To provide for calling forth the Militia (police,etc) to suppress Insurrections!! Nicely wrapped to protect the queen and all the queens' men!! What an armored Trojan horse in the Constitution. The Founding Fathers were protecting King William I's dream of the city of London and all the interest it would rake into his future coffers. And here we are 1,000 years later still under the British monarchy!!

Here we are pissing away all of our young American men and woman soldiers' lives, fortunes and families, so the queen dictator can live WITH HER LAZY GOLD LINED LIP SUCKING BANKERS in her fracking stone faced, fortified, moat, CASTLE!! While our veterans widows, sons and daughters wonder if they will be able to eat supper tonight or have a roof over their heads in the morning.

We did it in 1776 and 1812. When are we going to learn the left over one third Loyalists to King George III haven't left our country and are still fracking with us,, using us to gain world dominance over every fracking country, THEY THINK THEY OWN --------FROM THE U.S. TO CANADA, TO NEW ZEALAND, TO AUSTRAILA right down to the poor fracking farmers down in Grenada and the Falkland Islands.

The British Empire is using the U.S. and betting on the strength of the U.S. CONSTITUTION and our resources to conquer the world. With one nation, under the Queen, indivisible with no liberty and certainly no justice to all – JUST ASK LADY DIANA!!

Under Article I Section 10 #1 No State shall enter into any Treaty, Alliance. Or Confederation; grant Letter of Marque and Reprisal; coin Money; emit Bills of Credit; and make any Thing, but gold and silver Coin a Tender in Payment of Debts,etc.

This all disappears, when the U.S. PRINTING OFFICE cranked up the "FIAT" paper money machine to debase the currency and run inflation to the OMEGA!!

CHAPTER 18
THE INFAMOUS ELECTORAL COLLEGE

T HE ELECTORAL COLLEGE WAS INVENTED TO SHIFT THE FOCUS FROM THE CITIZENS' DIRECT POPULAR VOTE COUNT AND TO CONCEAL THROUGH FALSIFICATION AN UNBRIDLED INTENTION BY THE FOUNDERS TO KEEP POWER AND CONTROL.

THE REASONS GIVEN FOR THE ELECTORAL COLLEGE, ARE FEW AND FAR BETWEEN. THE PROPOSAL, THAT THE PEOPLE ELECT THE PRESIDENT WAS SOUNDLY REJECTED BY THE FOUNDING FATHERS, WHO WERE IN FAVOR OF INDIRECT POPULAR ELECTION. THEY JUST WANTED TO ATTEMPT TO CONTROL THE PRESIDENCY THROUGH POLITICAL MANIPULATION, LIKE – WE GOT YOU ELECTED AND THIS IS WHAT WE WANT!!

ONE HEDIOUS ARGUMENT AGAINST SCRAPPING THE ELECTORAL COLLEGE AT THE TIME

OF ITS INCEPTION, CLAIMS THAT DIRECT ELECTION MIGHT ENCOURAGE THIRD AND FOURTH PARTIES TO RISE UP TO BAT. WHAT A CROCK OF B.S. OBVIOUSLY, THOSE PEOPLE ARE PROPONENTS OF POWER AND CONTROL.

DIRECT DEMOCRACY (PURE DEMOCRACY), WAS OUR SCREEMING EAGLE, IT WAS DENOUNCED BY THE FOUNDING FATHERS AS MOB RULE!!

THE ELECTOR SYSTEM WAS DRAWN UP, BEHIND CLOSED DOORS AND RUBBER STAMPED BY A SPECIAL HAND PICKED COMMITTEE, WHICH REPRESENTED ONLY 12 COLONIAL STATES, SINCE PEOPLE IN RHODE ISLAND REFUSED TO PARTICIPATE IN THE SCAM! WE WERE NOT TRULY REPRESENTED IN 1787 AND TODAY, WE ARE NOT IN THE LEAST SENSE REPRESENTED THROUGH TRANSPARENCY.

AND NOW, ACCORDING TO MAUREEN DOWD WHO IS A COLUMNIST FOR THE NEW YORK TIMES WE HAVE CANDIDATE " ROMNEY WHO IS SO SECRETIVE THAT HE'S BEGINNING TO MAKE THE UBER-CLANDESTINE CHENEY LOOK LIKE THE BACHELORETTE".

"The Boston Globe reported on 7/24/2012 that although Romney promised "complete transparency" when he stepped in to save the Salt Lake City Olympics, he became a black hole:

"Some who worked with Romney describe a close –to-the-vest chief executive unwilling to share so much as a budget with a state board responsible for spending oversight. Archivists now say most key records about the Games' internal workings were destroyed under the supervision of a staffer shortly after the flame was extinguished at Olympic Cauldron Park, after Romney had returned to Massachusetts." (wouldn't it have been simpler to just burn the records in the flame?)" 1 All this comes from a man who had four deferments to keep himself out of Vietnam and would be considered a coward. None of his five sons, have volunteered for the military. So, this type of commander-in-chief would say-"Do as I say, not as I do and UPHOLD THE CONSTITUTION". The Electoral College would be good to this candidate, even if his head was stuck in sand.

IN ESSENCE THE FOUNDERS SABOTAGED THE POPULAR DIRECT DEMOCRATIC VOTE(MOST TOTAL VOTES IN AN ELECTION).

THE FOUNDERS MESMERIZED THE PUBLIC INTO THINKING, AN ALTERNATE PATHWAY TO PRESERVING DEMOCRACY WAS IMMEDIATE GRADIFICATION THROUGH SENSATIONALISM, NOT DEFAULT.

THE 2000 BUSH/GORE ELECTION AND PRE-VIOUS ELECTIONS HAVE PROVEN THAT THE ELECTORAL COLLEGE IS A FORMALITY, BASED UPON AN ELECTION GRAB, AS LONG AS YOU

HAVE THE 5/4 SUPREME COURT MAJJORITY IN YOUR BACK POCKET!

THE FOUNDERS BIGGEST FEAR WAS— IF WE GIVE A BLACK SLAVE A BOOK, WE WILL GET A BARACK OBAMA!!!

THE FOUNDERS WERE GOING TO HAVE IT THEIR WAY, NO MATTER WHAT THE COST AND USED EUPHEMISM TO DISTINGUISH THE FLAMES OF INJUSTICE!

IT IS TIME TO ABOLISH THE ELECTORAL COLLEGE AND PUT TERM LIMITS ON THE AUTOCRATIC THINKERS, WHO CREATED THE BIGGEST FINANCIAL MESS THIS COUNTRY HAS EVER SEEN.

FORGET THE LIBERALISM, FORGET THE CONSERVATISM, LETS GET BACK TO REAL AMERICANISM OR EQUALITY UNDER THE LAWS OF THE REPUBLIC IT WAS INTENDED TO BE!!

CHAPTER 19

"HOW FREE ARE WE ON THIS FOURTH OF JULY?"

The following views expressed are those of the Las Vegas Review-Journal on July 4, 2012

The Editorial

"How are we doing, safeguarding those "unalienable Rights" with which we are "endowed by our Creator" – in support of which 56 patriots solemnly pledged their lives, their fortunes and their sacred Honor, 236 years ago?

We remain free by many measures. Americans can still pretty much live where we want, work where we want, drive where we want. In fact, for women and racial minorities, those liberties have actually expanded over the past 70 years. We can all be proud of that.

But the average Southern Nevadan can be excused for sensing that the government now constricts like a boa around many of our remaining freedoms.

The cameras at every major intersection will only be used to spot traffic tie-ups, we're assured.

Police helicopters fly circles over our homes, shining spotlights into our backyards at night.

Now we're told the very kinds of robot drones used to assassinate terrorists overseas will be used by domestic police agencies, as well, presumably checking to see if junior has some pot planted out back.

Helmet and seat belt laws are justified by the costs of medical care to the Great Collective if you screw up. But you can't get an exemption by showing you've got good insurance or enough cash to pay for your own medical care, can you?

> Talking on a cell phone while you drive is now banned – so police complain people endanger other drivers by swerving off the road to answer an emergency call when a child is home alone.

> Signed into law by President Obama six months ago, the Defense Authorization Act "codifies into law the indefinite detention of terrorism suspects without trial" and authorizes the military to "carry out domestic anti-terrorism operations on U.S. soil," reports Erik Kain in Forbes magazine. The act authorizes the military to detain even U.S. citizens, again without trial.

> Mr. Kain of Forbes also warns about "other civil-liberty –quashing bills like the Sop Online Piracy Act and the Protect IP Act, two bills ...which would give the government and the industry sponsors ...

broad new powers over the Internet and freedom of speech online."

On May 9, FBI Director Robert Mueller "strongly recommended that Congress reauthorize the 2008 Foreign Intelligence Surveillance Act Amendments Act by the end of the year," writes Nat Hentoff. "This law allows federal authorities, including the FBI, to conduct warrantless searches." How did we get to this dangerous point?

It's been almost a century since minority President Woodrow Wilson ushered in the 1913-1921 "Progressive" era, from which sprouted many of these now expansive restraints on our freedoms.

First, there's the financial strip-search of the federal income tax. No person of modest means can open a bank account today that's immune to search by any IRS agent, who already has your Social Security or Employer Identification number. Obama Care authorizes thousands of new IRS agents with expanded "lien and levy" powers to do that searching.

Even today's massive and freedom-eating War on Drugs had its beginnings in the 1914 Harrison Narcotics Act, sold as a mere "truth in labeling law" that would never interfere with the right of Americans to buy painkillers or the right of doctors to prescribe them.

"He has abdicated Government here, by declaring us out of his Protection and waging War against us," the Founders wrote in their indictment of King George, back in 1776.

Our Constitution grants the federal government no authority to regulate drugs or medicine. So how did we end up with half a million Americans locked up for drug crimes, a disproportionate number of them blacks and Hispanics? This is no accident-the drugs banned were those most popular with black, Asian and Hispanic minorities 80 years ago, while the far more unhealthful booze and tobacco favored by white folk got a pass.

(Not that tobacco appears to be long for this world, though that's another story)

Meantime, is anyone surprised that the American Cancer Society laments the under-medication of cancer pain among terminal patients when doctors are scared they may be stripped of their livelihood for prescribing "too many" painkillers?

SWARMS OF OFFICERS'

Another of the colonists' complaints about King George was that he had "erected a multitude of New Offices, and sent hither swarms of Officers to harass our people, and eat out their substance."

Today's politicians pretend there's some mystery about why the American economy no longer produces enough jobs. What mystery?

Americans are an entrepreneurial people. Many of today's most successful corporations started as mom-and-pop operations, or with a couple of tinkerers building computers in a garage.

As demand for fledgling product or service grows it used to be natural to set up a brick-and-mortar workplace and hire employees.

But talk to anyone who's tried to set up such a business in recent years. It requires a wall full of licenses and permits, none of which come in a Cracker Jack box. The would-be businessman or woman is indeed "swarmed" with regulators, inspectors and tax men.

When you hire your first employee, you quickly learn you've just been dragooned as an uncompensated tax collector, obliged (on penalty of fines or jail should you get it wrong) to match withheld payroll taxes out of your own pocket –whether your fledgling business has ever shown a penny of profit, or not.

Soon the OSHA inspectors arrive. After all, there are quotas to reach. Then the ADA and the EPA come into play, "checking their common sense at the door," as one local politician puts it.

Next the state licensing boards lie in wait- thinly disguised protection rackets in which the very people whose market share you hope to steal away with your superior product or service get to decide whether you"re qualified to compete with them.

BY A MOCK TRIAL'

The signers of the declaration objected to the kind "quartering large bodies of armed troops among us" and " protecting them, by a mock Trial, from punishment for any Murders which they should commit on the Inhabitants of these States."

How many unarmed people have been shot and killed by Las Vegas police in recent years? Look up Orlando Barlow and Stanley Gibson for starters. How many of those shooters ever went to trial or even paid a fine? What shall we call the not-open-to-the-public processes that "cleared" them, if not "mock trials"?

Most of the redcoats who killed five in the Boston Massacre of 1770 were acquitted – John Adams defended – but at least there was a public trial.

The Fourth Amendment, written with the conduct of King George's men in mind, guarantees us "The right of the people to be secure in their persons, houses, papers, and effects, against unreasonable searches and seizures," etc.

Tried to board a commercial airliner lately? Did the TSA agents show you a warrant? Did they explain to you any probable cause to suspect you were engaged in criminal activity? Of course not. "But that's to protect our safety because we're at war with the terrorists."

Who's the enemy? The current administration won't even admit Maj. Nidal Hasan, charged with killing a dozen men for whom he was responsible at Fort Hood, Texas, in 2009, is a Muslim Jihadist. They simply call him a mentally ill person whose motives remain unimaginable.

But even the pragmatic argument that this keeps us safe fails. Though the TSA struggles to keep the reports under wraps, government auditors repeatedly give the TSA miserable grades when they try to sneak weapons through the screenings.

The attacks of Sept.11, 2001, would likely never have been brought to fruition had a reasonable number of passengers been carrying their own concealed firearms_ the only solution allowed by the Second Amendment, with its absolute decree that "The right of the people to keep and bear arms shall not be infringed."

And now, as of last week, the Supreme Court has ruled there's no "mandate" for an individual to buy health insurance, but we nonetheless have a right to see our neighbors taxed to pay for our health care, even if we live on beer and Twinkies.

Since this creates a disincentive to take care of our own health – instead encouraging us to rely on the government to tax our neighbors to pay our medical bills - watch for government to soon move to take away more free choices in this area, attempting for starters to ban sugary soda pop and fried foods. Oh, wait ..." 1

My commentary and review to The Editorial can be summoned up in ten words, "God Bless America, We are going to need your blessings".

CHAPTER 20

REMEMBER THE FALKLAND ISLANDS

Why are the Falkland Islands so close to America's future and what do they have to do with our Constitution? Read on- FACT OR FICTION?

"The Argentines' identity also is wrapped up in their historic claim against the British, which dates to the republic's founding.

The French settled the islands first, in 1764, naming them Iles Malouines, which the Spanish translated as Las Malvinas. A year later, the British established a settlement there, claiming the islands as their own, without realizing the French were already there, on the other side of the archipelago. Their dispute, and many others, continued until 1833, when the British navy definitively took control.

A few years earlier, in its campaigns against Spain, Britain attacked Buenos Aires. Memories of British troops in the capital were raw as Argentina became a nation. And ever since, Argentines have considered the islands their lost province, a vestige of colonial power they believe Britain STOLE

FROM THEM after ousting the South Americans who had been there."

My point is the British are on a globalization kick and they won't let go. America is their next prime target and they are doing a pretty damn good job of ousting North Americans who lived there. They have gobbled up most of the prime property in Kauai (Princeville-notice the solid name Princeville), Hawaii and the other Hawaiian Islands. EVEN THE STATE OF HAWAII FLAG LOOKS LIKE THE FLAG OF GREAT BRITAIN!! They have named and renamed towns, cities, counties and streets all over America after their ancestors. They flood millions of dollars annually into the coffers of candidates who support their way of thinking to keep the monarch alive and extending. THEY HAVE USED THE POWER AND MIGHT OF AMERICA TO FURTHER THEIR GLOBALIZA-TION AGENDA, WITH LITTLE RISK OF THEIR OWN COUNTRYMEN.

OUR SOLDIERS HAVE BEEN A PAWN IN THE MONARCH'S QUEST FOR WORLD POWER AND DENOMINATION AT WHATEVER THE COST! THE U.S. CONSTITUTION BY ITS POWER AND CONTROL IS THE VEHICLE THAT WILL GET THEM TO WHERE THEY ARE GOING AND BEYOND!

Friedrich Nietzsche, the German philosopher, said it all in the "Dawn" published in 1881, "THE SUREST WAY

TO CORRUPT A YOUTH IS TO INSTRUCT HIM/
HER TO HOLD IN HIGHER ESTEEM, THOSE
WHO THINK ALIKE, RATHER THAN THOSE WHO
THINK DIFFERENTLY."

America's children are being brain washed into thinking that they are free, when real freedom has never reached
its shores. The only thing that has over reached its shores is
BRITISH IMPERIALISM!

The Founders of the Constitution have transported and
supported the very same idealism they supposedly rejected.
They infiltrated YOUR property rights and gave them to a
ghost. Today, our government has allowed such frivolous
instruments e.g. MERS- mortgage electronic REGISTRA-
TION system to come into play augmenting GSE'S – GOV-
ERNMENT SPONSERED ENTERPRISES (FANNIE
MAE AND FREDDIE MAC, FHA, VA,ETC) TO HELP
STEAL YOUR PROPERTY!

TODAY, Property titles are lost in cyberspace due to the
bundling and selling off of mortgage loans at a discount.
Credit DEFAULT SWAPS continue at a rapid pace to place
your personal residence in limbo for years to come. Derivatives
[which look like your son or daughters fractions section from
their ALGEBRA 2 TEXBOOK] are sold at bay and can be
attached to your property, without you having the least hint of
jeopardy!! By the way, what the hell is a derivative? The wall
street junkies INVENTED THESE DERIVATIVE CASH
COWS TO SELL OUT AMERICA AND ARE supported

by the BRITISH BANKERS, who want you to live in a constant state of CONFUSION, while they up heave the very property they INTEND TO OWN----FOREVER-----YOURS!![They want you to live in a tent like Chief Sitting Bull, until the day you die]

ACCORDING TO WARREN BUFFET, "DERIVATIVES ARE FINANCIAL WEAPONS OF MASS DESTRUCTION.....POTENTIALLY LETHAL".

CHAPTER 21
DECLARATION OF INDEPENDENCE (GONE & FORGOTTEN?)

Basic ideas about people and government have come back to haunt the Founders. Our rights to "life, liberty and property (which has been since changed to" the pursuit of happiness" to conceal their infamous 3/5 BLACK person invention and racism) have been usurped by government. e.g. (1) The Patriot Act, (2) The Supreme Court and lower courts position on "NO ORAL ARGUMENTS" BEFORE TRIAL UNLESS CHIEF JUSTICES SAY SO THERE IS NO MOBILITY, SINCE THEY ALSO DECIDE WHICH CASES ARE TO MOVE FORWARD AND WATCH FOR TELLTALE SIGNS OF THOSE CASES THAT MIGHT UPSET THE STATUS QUO e.g. BANK FRAUD & MORTGAGE FRAUD,(3) Police state (round up, aggravate, arrest citizens trying to voice an opposite opinion), (4) EMINENT DOMAIN –Just let the banksters "grab" your property, without filing proper paper work, e.g. assignments of mortgage note, deed of trust title, etc. etc.. The purpose of our government was suppose to protect these rights. B.S.

People are supposed to be the masters of government and not the other way around. Unfortunately, FASCISM has raised its ugly head and taken over America and once again, Our FOUNDERS have failed the litmus test. We all know that the only way people can change the government or get rid of it and create a new one, (in light of the present day "Nazi police state" is through uncivil means like we used in order to be free from British rule. Although we shouldn't condone this type of behavior, due to the extreme consequences it proposes, we should all remember that it was used historically. In other words – civil disobedience does have its dividends. It's not what you say, but how you say it!!!

Perhaps the complaints against the British King that the Founders listed were only superficial, in that they fell far short. Let's do a compare and contrast chart from 1776 and fast forward to 2012 (today), to see if the Founders were self serving or TROJAN horses in the king's garments!

-----RIGHTS VIOLATED -----

THEN (1776)	NOW (2012)
A. The king refused to approve laws made by the colonists for their common good	A The supreme court legislates Citizens United and Eminent Domain laws for their government control
B. The King closed the colonists legislatures when they opposed his violation of the people.	B The Patriot Acct takes away our Bill of Rights
C. The King kept a standing army in the colonies even though there was no war	C. Today, we keep a major swat team Ready to abuse our children and grandgrandc grandchildren's First Amendment Rights a Rights and hide an army of national gur guardsmen and police off in the shado shadows.
D. The King stopped the colonists trade with other countries	D. We shun Iran, Iraq, Venezuela, Cuba and others in the name of WMD's.
E. The king taxed the colonists without their consent.	E.WE ARE TAXED TO DEATH,PERIOD!
F. The king took away the colonists right to trial by jury.	F. Today, the chief justices of all

```
our----------------------our federal and state courts decide
w------------------------what cases move forward and no
ora---------------------oral arguments or discovery is heard
u------------------------unless the chief justice allows your
ca-----------------------case to "Proceed". The chief justice
is-----------------------is judge, jury and executioner all
wrap------------------wrapped up in one.No trial by jury as
r-------------------------requested. Trial on demand only.
```

Remember, many loyalists (those faithful to King George III) were large land owners or wealthy merchants. They thought their businesses would be hurt by independence. Today, those same loyalists are your members of the Federal Reserve System, who want war, war, war. Because they cash – in on Congressional approval of war to borrow our own money from the privately held Federal Reserve to support such demonous acts. Other loyalists to King George had been APPOINTED to their jobs by the king!! The same hold true today. Most JUDGES are appointed by the President, Governors of states, etc. IF THEY WERE ELECTED MANY WOULD LOSE THEIR JOBS FOR BEING BIAS OR INCOMPETENT.

THE 40 CLUB

Forty men signed The U.S. Constitution that was adopted on September 17, 1787. Today, this same constitution celebrates the control of over 330 million Americans. It's the law! Remember, 40 men put into law an outdated document that continues to give rise to the FASCIST government we encounter today!! Class warfare was the resultant force of the selfishly written words of men, who prescribed the powers "they" wanted to see enhance "their" vision or agendas, during "their" time, according to "their" own undeniable wealth and power to promote the power and control of the future masses of people to follow. And guess what? They were UNELECTED TO DO SO, and they did it behind CLOSED DOORS!!

CHAPTER 22
RANTS BY THE BUCKET LOADS

1. 1970'S BANKING DEREGULATION ALLOWS BANK OF AMERICA TO CROSS OVER STATE LINES INTO FLORIDA. THIS STARTED THE WHOLE MESS WE ARE IN TODAY....INTER-STATE BANKING

2. 1999 GRAM-LEACH-BILEY ACT OVERTURNS THE GLASS-STEAGALL ACT OF 1933 AND ALLOWS BANKS TO OFFER A MENU OF FINANCIAL SERVICES, INCLUDING INVEST-MENT BANKING AND INSURANCE SALES-NEW CASH COWS

3. THE FEDERAL RESERVE IS MASTER OF ALL THAT IT CONTROLS!!!!!

4. 9-11-2001 THE FED'S LOANED 45 BILLION TO FINANCIAL INSTITUTIONS, IN ORDER TO PROVIDE STABILITY TO THE U.S. ECON-OMY. YEAH RIGHT! FOR A PRICE TO GET TO CONTINUE INTEREST IN PERPETU-

ITY. ALWAYS AN INCIDENT TO REAP THE MONEY. THE FED PLAYED THE PIVOTAL ROLE – YES-THERE WAS SOMETHING IN IT FOR THEM –BILLIONS OF DOLLARS –LIQUID CASH FOR THE QUEEN!!

5. EXXON VALDEZ OIL SPILL DEBT FORGIVEN BY A FEDERAL JUDGE!!

6. NO BID CONTRACTS BY ENRON AND BETCHEL

7. NO POLITICS ON PUBLIC PROPERTY. IT IS ONLY O.K. IF YOU ARE A SITTING SENATOR

8. EMINENT DOMAIN MAKES SENSE AND COULD REDUCE YOUR PRINCIPLE!

9. DEL MAR RACE TRACK – LADIES HAT CONTEST LEAVES THE QUEEN WITH LITTLE TO DESIRE!

10. IF YOU PULL THE PLUG ON SUPER PAC MONEY, T.V. AND RADIO ADVERTISEMENT REVENUE WILL DRY UP!!

11. AMERICAN BAR ASSOCIATION – LIBERTY AND JUSTICE FOR ALL OR FOR THEMSELVES?

12. DID YOU EVER NOTICE THAT AMERICA'S INTERSTATE HIGHWAY SIGNS, ARE MADE IN THE FORM OF A SHIELD? THAT'S TO REMIND YOU THAT THE QUEENS SHIELD

OF HONOR IN BATTLE, REIGNS IN AMER-
ICA !!!

13. IF THE BRITISH STOLE IRELAND, WHO'S NEXT??

14. DID JOHN MCCAIN REALLY SING, "BOMB, BOMB,BOMB IRAN?"

15. "ASK NOT WHAT YOUR COUNTRY CAN DO FOR YOU, BUT WHAT YOU CAN DO FOR YOUR COUNTRY"

16. GOD, WE NEED TO SAVE OUR MONEY FOR THE QUEEN!

17. WILL SOMEBODY PLEASE TELL ME WHAT THE FRACK A DERIVATIVE IS?

18. DAD...............".IT'S A QUADRATIC EQUA-TION TAKEN RIGHT OUT OF MY ALGEBRA 2 TEXT BOOK. LOOK I'M NOT KIDDING! THE INNOVATIVE WALL STREET BANKSTERS, SUBSTITUTED LETTERS FOR NUMBERS TO INVENT MONEY AND ANOTHER WAY TO SCREW US".!!

19. YEAH RIGHT, THEY SCREWED UP OUR MINDS AND THE COUNTRY!!

20. DAD.........WHAT'S A HEDGE FUND??

21. YOU'RE NEARING YOUR 21ST BIRTHDAY.... GO ASK MITT ROMNEY, I THINK IT MEAN S "WHO DO YOU WANT TO FRACK TODAY?"

22. "WE ARE VERY BAD AT PROSECUTING FINANCIAL CRIMES IN THIS COUNTRY," said Kenneth Clark, Britain's justice secretary.

23. SUPER-PACS ARE NEW GANGS, ACTING LIKE LITTLE KIDS IN A PLAYGROUND. THEY DESTROY REPUTATIONS AND ARE POWER HUNGRY FREAKS.

24. ARE TOP BANKERS IN AMERICA NOTHING MORE THAN WHITE-COLLAR CRIMINALS DISSEMINATING FRAUDULENT BONUSES THROUGH ACTS OF CONGRESS VIA TAX-PAYER BAILOUTS?

25. ARE POLTICAL BANKERS REALLY MOB GANGSTERS?

26. MITT ROMNEY SAYS, "BORROW MONEY FROM YOUR PARENTS FOR COLLEGE". (SO, IF THEY DEFAULT ON THE COLLEGE LOAN, WE CAN COME AND GRAB THEIR PROPERTY!!)

27. WHILE PARTYING IN LAS VEGAS, WAS PRINCE HARRY SENDING A MESSAGE FROM THE QUEEN TO THE U.S.?? (BEND OVER WERE HERE TO FRACK YOU!!)

CHAPTER 23
SOCRATES AND PLATO, ABSOLUTE TRUTH, GREECE (USA TAKE A LESSON)!

T HE Historical Context

1. Plato was born in Athens ca. 427 B.C. at the end of what is historically called the Golden Age of Athens or the Age of Pericles (ca. 445-431 B.C.).

2. Athens of this period is viewed as our ideal and model as the FIRST DEMOCRACY, and as a city DEVOTED to human excellence in mind and body.

3. By the 5th Century B.C.; Athens had become a democracy as the result of the struggle between a small number of land-owning families (of the aristocracy) and great numbers of the poor.

4. Most of the prominent and influential citizens of Athens were democratic or had become democratic in their political views.

5. THE ATHENIAN STATE HAD A CONSTITUTION AND A SUPREME COURT, WHICH

INCORPORATED A JURY SYSTEM OF 6,000 JURORS, DIVIDED INTO PANELS, AND FORMED THE BASIS OF ATHENIAN DEMOCRACY.

a. ALL citizens were EQUAL under the law, in basic education, and in political life through direct DEMOCRATIC DEBATE AND VOTING.

b. There was FREEDOM OF SPEECH and HUMANE TREATMENT of aliens (metics) and SLAVES.

c. The city GOVERNMENT WAS VIEWED AS A MODEL OF JUSTICE for the known WORLD and Athenians had FEELINGS OF INTENSE PRIDE AND LOYALTY FOR THE CITY ITSELF.1

NOW, FAST FORWARD THE ABOVE THINKING TO THE AMERICA WE LIVE IN TODAY AND MATCH OUR MEANING OF DEMOCRACY! WHAT'S MISSING?

1. WE ARE NOW IN A GOLDEN AGE IN WHICH OUR LEADERS DO NOT SAY, WHERE DO YOU WANT TO GO TODAY, BUT SAY WHO CAN WE FRACT TODAY!

2. America is viewed as the POSTER CHILD FOR GREAT BRITAIN'S WORLD GLOBALIZATION!

3. TODAY IN AMERICA, THE BILL OF RIGHTS HAS BEEN TRASHED AND HAS BECOME DEBT INTEREST OWED TO GREAT BRITAIN'S RUTHLESS BANKERS!

4. MOST OF OUR PROMINENT AND INFLUENTIAL LEADERS HAVE SOLD THEIR SOUL TO POLITICAL CONVENTION, THAT DEMEANS ALL OTHER DIFFERENCE OF OPINION!

5. WE CRY "DEMOCRACY", BUT ALL OF OUR CITIZENS ARE NOT EQUAL under the law through DEBATE AND VOTING!

6. THERE IS NO "ABSOLUTE"2 FREEDOM OF SPEECH and NO HUMANE TREATMENT OF OUR OCCUPY WALL STREET OR OTHER MOVEMENTS THAT TRUTHFULLY EXPRESS A DIFFERENCE OF OPINION!

7. OUR CONGRESS AND SUPREME COURT IS NOT VIEWED AS A MODEL OF JUSTICE FOR THE WORLD AND WE DO NOT HAVE FEELINGS OF INTENSE PRIDE AND LOYALTY FOR OUR COUNTRY, SINCE JUSTICE IN AMERICA WAS D.O.A.(DEAD ON ARRIVAL) AT THE PHILADELPHIA CONVENTION IN 1776 AND BEYOND!

CHAPTER 24
SITTING BULL, AN AMERICAN PATRIOT

Despite all that has been written about Sitting Bull, he was a true patriot to North America. Born hear the Grand River in Dakota Territory, he was killed by Indian agency police on the Standing Rock Indian Reservation during an attempt to arrest him and prevent him from supporting the Ghost Dance movement.

Guess what? Sitting Bull you are not forgotten! The BACK END OF AMERICA IS RISING! Chief Sitting Bull was only trying to protect his NATIVE AMERICAN FAMILY and PROPERTY, WHICH WAS BEING STOLEN FROM HIM, by British settlers, who were really only after the GOLD they heard about in the Black Hills and in California. In 1874, Lt. Col. George Armstrong Custer's announcement of gold in the Black Hills, TRIGGERED the Black Hills Gold Rush.1 Tensions increased between Chief Sitting Bull's Sioux and EUROPEAN AMERICANS WHO WERE ONLY THERE TO STEAL HIS FRACKING PROPERTY! Ask, yourself, wouldn't you resist if some bankster, didn't have title to your property?(All this happened within 297 years from the date, that Queen Elizabeth sent Francis Drake to America (1577) to STEAL THE GOLD! SO, THERE IS A PATTERN TO STEAL AMERICA'S WEALTH LIKE A SHELL COMPANY SET UP TO DEFRAUD YOU!

Sitting Bull had a premonition of defeating the cavalry, which motivated his Native American people to a major victory at the Battle of the Little Bighorn against Lt. Col. George Armstrong Custer and the 7th Cavalry on June 25, 1876. Months after the battle, Sitting Bull and his group left the United States to Wood Mountain, Saskatchewan, where he remained until 1881, at which time he surrendered to U.S. forcesl.2

Only because of fears that he would use his influence to support the Ghost Dance movement, Indian Service agent James McLaughlin at Fort Yates ordered his arrest. During an ensuing struggle between Sitting Bull's followers and the agency police, SITTING BULL WAS SHOT AND KILLED, IN FRONT OF HIS OWN FAMILY, IN HIS OWN KITCHEN, IN HIS OWN HOME!

But, the whole story doesn't end there. In the Dakota War of 1862 several bands of the Sioux killed 600 settlers and soldiers in south-central Minnesota in response to POOR TREATMENT BY THE GOVERNMENT AND IN AN EFFORT TO DRIVE THE WHITES AWAY!

Sitting Bull's band of Hunkpapa continued to attack migrating parties and forts in the late 1860's. When in 1871 the NORTHERN PACIFIC RAILWAY conducted a survey for a route across the northern plains directly through Hunkpapa lands, it encountered stiff Sioux resistance. The same railway people returned the following year accompanied by federal troops.

The Lakota coalition of which Sitting Bull was the ostensible head, was the PRIMARY TARGET OF THE FEDERAL GOVERNMENT'S PACIFICATION CAMPAIGN.

This is an American tragedy, but its example is not only horrific and applies to the taking of one man's property only to steal the mineral rights under it!

CHIEF SITTING BULL, MAY YOU REST IN PEACE AND ALL THE SOULS OF YOUR DEPARTED HEAR THE "GHOST DANCE" FROM THE HEAVENS ABOVE.

During the "GHOST DANCE" Sitting Bull was only praying to his god to help him save his family and people!

ABOUT THE BOOK
FACT OR FICTION – YOU DECIDE!

I hope I have humored all the pragmatist, who's wistful thinking[that also played Saran Palin and all who have come before the storm] is all but imaginational dream.

Leonard Pitts who is a columnist for the Miami Herald said, "To score Palin for being unfactual, then, is to bring boxing gloves to a knife fight. The death panels are not about fact. They are about fear and the shameless manipulation thereof for political gain. The thought of which is that Americans increasingly occupy two realities, one based on the conviction that facts matter, the other on the notion that facts are only what you need them to be in a given moment. That ought to give all of us pause because it leads somewhere we should not want to go. When two realities divide one people, the outcome seems obvious. They cannot remain one people."

I sincerely hope I have presented a different point of view.

Ralph Waldo Emerson said it best, when confronted with the question – what is the meaning of life? He responded, "TO LAUGH OFTEN AND MUCH, TO WIN THE

RESPECT OF INTELLIGENT PEOPLE, TO EARN THE AFFECTION OF CHILDREN, TO ENDURE THE BETRAYAL OF FALSE FRIENDS, TO LEAVE THIS LIFE A BIT BETTER, WHETHER BY A HEALTHY CHILD, A GARDEN PATCH, OR A REDEEMED SOCIAL CONDITION, THIS IS TO HAVE MASTERED THE MEANING OF LIFE."

One Founding Father said it for all posterity to hear:

"An appeal to arms and to the God of hosts is all that is left us!...Sir, we are not weak if we make a proper use of those means which the God of nature hath placed in our power... Besides, sir, we shall not fight our battles alone. There is a just God who presides over the destinies of nations and who will raise up friends to fight our battles for us... Is life so dear, or peace so sweet as to be purchased at the price of chains and slavery? Forbid it, Almighty God! I know not what course others may take; but as for me, give me liberty or give me death!" by Patrick Henry: Patriot and Statesman

America is undoubtedly the greatest nation on earth. However, to nail the sign "IN GOD WE TRUST" in the hallowed halls of its Congress is an understatement. It is going to take more than a few words to convince the American people that their leaders really can be TRUSTED, beyond euphemism. Instead of "We bailed the banks out, they sold us out" let us unite once again and chant, "GOD BLESS AMERICA", so loud that Kate Smith, hears us above the fruited plains.

NOTES
PREFACE

1. - "We the People" Center of Civic Education 1988 ISBN 0-89818-108-9 P.33 #4
2. Ibid P.33

CHAPTER 2-THE UBLY, THE BAD, THE GOOD

1. -E.J. DIONNE, WASHINGTON POST "Opponents are now "moving" Obama to Europe. LAS VEGAS SUN 1/16/2012 p.3
2. -"IN GOD WE TRUST"-JAMES MADISON, LAS VEGAS REVIEW JOURNAL 7/04/2012 p.8A BY www.hobbylobby.com/ministry projects Need Him Ministry, Oklahoma City,OK

CHAPTER 4-VAULTING ACROSS THE ATLANTIC

1. THE WEIGH OF VENGEANCE", THE UNITED STATES, THE BRITISH EMPIRE, AND THE WAR OF 1812. TROY BICKHAM, OXFORD UNIVERSITY PRESS

CHAPTER 5- PROBLEMS DIRECTLY AND INDIRECTLY RELATED TO THE CONSTITUTION

1. DAVID STRINGER AND JILL LAWLESS-BROWN, THE ASSOCIATED PRESS 4/06/2010, LAS VEGAS REVIEW –JOURNAL P.8A

CHAPTER 12-FREEDOM OF EXPRESSION

1. "WE THE PEOPLE", THE CITIZEN AND THE CONSTITUTION, CENTER FOR CIVIC EDU-CATION, 2003, L-1 ISBN 0-89818-169-0 P.140,141
2. WWW. HUFFINGTON POST.COM/2008/10/06 MCCAIN-OBAMA HATRED AT MC CAIN-PALIN RALLIES! "TERRORIST!" "KILL HIM!" (VIDEO). ALSO, FROM THE WASHINGTON POST AND AMERICA BLOG ON PALIN'S RALLY, http://www.jackandjillpolitics.com/2008/10when-theirsuppporter-call-oba7/28/2012
3. 'WE THE PEOPLE". THE CITIZEN AND THE CONSTITUTION, CENTER FOR CIVIC EDU-CATION, 2003, L-1 ISBN 0-89818-169-0 P.136,137

CHAPTER 13-FREEDOM OF SPEECH FROM THE FCC, WITH LOVE!

1. KKRP AM1610 LISTEN TO MY READIO.COM. FCC DEREGULATION, STAR COM MEDIA LLC COWLINGTON, OKLAHOMA

CHAPTER 14-THE SUPREME COURT TO THE PEOPLE OF MONTANA-GO TO HELL, YOU'RE S__T OUT OF LUCK!

1. ROBERT BARNES, THE WASHINGTON POST, "COURT'S RULING REAFFIRMS CITIZEN UNITED DECISION", LAS VEGAS REVIEW-JOURNAL 6/26/2012 P. 7A
2. IBID. P7A

CHAPTER 15- A SYNOPSIS FROM GLADSTONE

1. BARTON FAMILY OF FUNERAL SERVICE, KING, PIERCE AND SNOHOM COUNTIES, WESTERN WASHINGTON STATE, BARTON-FUNERAL.COM, FUNERAL BASICS, SIR WILLIAM GLADSTONE 1809-1898
2. CRAIG WHITLOCK AND GREG JAFFE, THE WASHINGTON POST. DOVER AIR FORCE BASE MORTUARY, LAS VEGAS REVIEW-JOURNAL 11/10/2011 P. 6A

CHAPTER 18- THE INFAMOUS ELECTORAL COLLEGE

1. MAUREEN DOWD, THE NEW YORK TIMES, AS REPORTED IN THE BOSTON GLOBE –

MITT ROMNEY: HIDING IN PLAIN SIGHT, LAS VEGAS SUN 7/26/2012 OPINION 3

CHAPTER 19- HOW FREE ARE WE?

1. EDITORIAL,THE LAS VEGAS REVIEW-JOURNAL 7/04/2012 HOW FREE ARE WE ON THIS FOURTH OF JULY?

CHAPTER 23- SOCRATES AND PLATO, ABSOLUTE TRUTH, GREECE (USA TAKE A LESSON)!

1. http://en.wikipedia.orgo/wiki/phaedo
2. http://www.hoocher.com/Philosophy/plato.htm

CHAPTER 24-CHIEF SITTING BULL, AN AMERICAN PATRIOT

1. Http://en.wikipedia.org/wiki/Sitting_Bull
2. IBID

ABOUT THE BOOK-FACT OR FICTION- YOU DECIDE!

www.ingramcontent.com/pod-product-compliance
Lightning Source LLC
Chambersburg PA
CBHW020438290526
45785CB00002B/900